Making Failure Pay

MAKING failure PAY

For-Profit Tutoring, High-Stakes Testing, and Public Schools

JILL P. KOYAMA

The University of Chicago Press :: Chicago and London

JILL P. KOYAMA is assistant professor in the Graduate School of Education at University at Buffalo–SUNY.

The University of Chicago Press, Chicago 60637
The University of Chicago Press, Ltd., London
© 2010 by The University of Chicago
All rights reserved. Published 2010
Printed in the United States of America

19 18 17 16 15 14 13 12 11 10   1 2 3 4 5

ISBN-13: 978-0-226-45173-2   (cloth)
ISBN-13: 978-0-226-45174-9   (paper)
ISBN-10: 0-226-45173-9   (cloth)
ISBN-10: 0-226-45174-7   (paper)

Library of Congress Cataloging-in-Publication Data

Koyama, Jill Peterson.
    Making failure pay : for-profit tutoring, high-stakes testing, and public schools / Jill P. Koyama.
        p. cm.
    Includes bibliographical references and index.
    ISBN-13: 978-0-226-45173-2 (cloth: alk. paper)
    ISBN-13: 978-0-226-45174-9 (pbk.: alk. paper)
    ISBN-10: 0-226-45173-9 (cloth: alk. paper)
    ISBN-10: 0-226-45174-7 (pbk.: alk. paper) 1. United States. No Child Left Behind Act
of 2001. 2. School improvement programs—Government policy—United States. 3. Educational accountability—United States. 4. Privatization in education—United States.
5. Education—Standards—United States. 6. Education and state—United States. 7. Public
schools—United States. I. Title.
    LB2822.82.K69 2010
    379.1—dc22
                                                                            2009047691

♾ The paper used in this publication meets the minimum requirements of the American
National Standard for Information Sciences—Permanence of Paper for Printed Library
Materials, ANSI Z39.48-1992.

Be equally indifferent to success and failure.

KRISHNA BHAGAVAD-GITA,
chapter 4, verse 22

Failure was the badly trained dog that lived in other people's houses.

RANI MANICKA

Failure is gray, smudging whatever it touches.

SCOTT SANDAGE

As a cultural fact, the success/failure complex will have its say.

HERVÉ VARENNE, SHELLEY GOLDMAN, and
RAY MCDERMOTT

CONTENTS

ACKNOWLEDGMENTS

Working in the field and writing as an anthropologist, though engaging, can also be isolating. Aloneness, however, need not be more than temporary. I was fortunate, throughout my research, often to be in the company of encouraging others. I am grateful to the people, animals, places, and things—Latour's human and nonhuman "mediators"—that kept me thinking, exploring, and writing. They were numerous. The people in my life endured the "preoccupied" me—the person who cancelled dinner plans so she could write, who was consumed with ideas and analysis when attending theater, and who repeatedly interrupted otherwise reciprocal conversations with long musings about actor-network theory. My friends and family were unsparing in their patience, understanding, and compassion. Thank you.

No book should be considered an individual achievement, and I take this work to be one result of my ongoing engagement with the ideas and work of many students and colleagues. I make special mention of four people. For many years, Hervé Varenne has consistently questioned that which had been considered unquestionable in the subfield of anthropology and education; as my advisor, he encouraged, if not gently commanded, me to do likewise. I acknowledge his incredible influence and generous intellectual support. I thank Lesley Bartlett for providing me with multiple contexts in which I could develop and share my research. She, as much as anyone, is responsible for my growth as an educator and as an anthropologist. Margaret (Greta) Gibson has been an unending source of guidance. Working with Greta, I developed a respect for anthropological inquiry. I also thank Ofelia García, for mentoring me, befriending me, challenging my ideas, and sharing her academic bilingual world.

Ethnographies, once conducted and written, become books because of editors. I thank Elizabeth Branch Dyson, my editor. I met Elizabeth at an annual meeting of the American Anthropological Association. Her insight, intelligence, and warmth were evident during our first meeting, and I became committed to working with her and the accomplished staff at the University of Chicago Press, including Anne Goldberg and Mark Reschke. I am grateful to Edmund (Ted) Hamann and his student, Jennifer Nelson, who through reviews procured by Elizabeth, offered useful insights, asked provocative questions, and provided poignant suggestions. I also thank a third anonymous reviewer. The critiques of all three dramatically improved this final version of *Making Failure Pay*.

To my colleagues, staff, and students at University at Buffalo, The State University of New York, I offer praise and thanks. Their questions propel my thinking. Their scholarship inspires my curiosity. And their support for my work encourages my research. I am incredibly fortunate to participate in a collective with such warm, interesting, and intelligent people.

And finally, my gratitude to Elly. She gave much time to read, discuss, and edit multiple versions of this book. More importantly, it is because of her that I have come to know that the important moments are, not the greatest achievements, but the less prepossessing—the ongoing, everyday interactions in a shared life.

ENGAGING FAILURE

Probing the Problematics and Politics of Policy

Scenario 1: Attending a Supplemental Educational Services Fair

On a hot and humid evening in late September 2005, booths, balloons, and brochures—all filled with promises of benefiting failing schools and their failing students—are readied for the night's event. I watch as principals, assistant principals, and parent coordinators of New York City's failing schools trickle into the decorated space, a gymnasium of a Brooklyn high school. The booth attendants—mostly well-dressed managers and marketers of the 132 tutoring companies approved by the state—turn their attentions away from their tables and balloons to greet groups of arrivals with requisite small talk and offers of promotional materials, sample curricula, and mission statements. Hands are shaken. Smiles are exchanged. Parent coordinators linger at each booth, building their cache of promotional key chains, pens, identification holders, and stringed backpacks. Most principals do not linger; they talk on their cellular phones, direct their parent coordinators to particular booths, nibble on snacks provided by the host school, and talk to each other, comparing their school's failing status to those of their colleagues.

Under the federal education policy, No Child Left Behind (NCLB), all of the principals are in similar situations. They each lead a school that has been deemed to be in some state of "failure."[1] Of course there are notable differences. Some of their schools have already been marked for "reconstitution" or "restructuring," while others have just begun the initial descent of educational remedial rehabilitation for schools in need of improvement (SINI). A few are in between, in "corrective action" (U.S. Department of Education 2001). Still, all the principals attend the night's event because they can and they must. They have been selected from among the large pool of school administrators across the city, invited because of their schools' inabilities or failures to increase academic achievement. There will be more events like this one, throughout late autumn and into early winter, but many principals have decided to attend tonight, near the beginning of the school year.

Conversations quickly turn to unmet benchmarks, low test scores, achievement gaps, elevated passing score requirements, and teachers who refuse to teach test preparation—all signs of possible (but not certain) school failure. The principals dutifully comment on their inability to meet the state's adequate yearly progress (AYP) toward proficiency for at least three consecutive years. From the principals' conversations, I learn that "too many special needs students really drag down AYPs" and "getting rid of students who will probably drop out anyway really helps the numbers." One principal hopes aloud that his "worst students" will transfer to other schools.

Scenario 2: Increasing Principal Accountability

The demands are many for the principal of Brooklyn's Middle School (MS) 200, an administrator I'd met at the August fair.[2] She has worked for twenty years at the same school, first as a teacher, then as an assistant principal, and for the last seven as a principal. Throughout her career, she tells me in an interview conducted at MS 200, she has found herself responsible for implementing new federal and state policies in the school. Yet, as retirement nears, she sees herself as nearly singularly accountable for the outcomes measured by NCLB and New York City's Children First reforms, which in her words, "get in the way of each other."

The principal is overwhelmed when we talk eight months after the supplemental educational services (SES) fair, in March 2006. Implementing federal, state, and district policies, she explains, "always comes down to schools and the people who run them." She speaks about the lack of support from the city's central Department of Education (DOE) offices. Being the buffer between the DOE and her staff is nothing new, but with limited support for implementing NCLB mandates, like SES, the tasks required by the federal policy daunt this principal. She is becoming increasingly accountable, and while she exhibits confidence in her administrative skills, she is unclear that her actions are making the necessary differences.

Since her school posted low test scores for English language learners (ELLs), and thus, failed to meet AYPs, the principal reorganized her classes and teachers.[3] She added small-group morning instruction for her lowest-scoring students and implemented afterschool tutoring for eligible students by contracting with United Education, a state-approved afterschool tutoring company.[4] Still, progress has been incredibly slow, and she expects her school to be moved into the next sanction level, "corrective action."

When asked specifically about SES, the principal admits that some of her students are probably benefiting from the tutoring in English language arts (ELA) and mathematics provided by United Education, but she objects to the notion that she needs help from an outside company to "turn her own school around." She also resents that public funds from her budget are being diverted from the school to the private services that United Education and other educational support companies, which are not directly accountable for improving test scores or meeting AYP goals, supply.

Scenario 3: Managing SES Programs

The United Education manager who supervises the SES program at MS 200 said he understood why principals in New York City, and, in fact, across the rest of the country, resist SES. Having the federal government tell you, via NCLB, that you don't know what you're doing and that you need the expertise of the educational support industry, he reasoned, would anger many principals he knows. Being labeled a "failing" or "low-performing" school is a stigma that carries consequences for principals.

However, when I interviewed the manager in United's Manhattan corporate office, he is convinced that if the schools had been "doing their jobs better all along, then there'd have been no need for NCLB or SES." The manager, who has been working for United Education for five years, knows that instituting anything in the education system takes time. It's June 2007 and the manager surmises that as students' test scores increase and schools emerge from their failing status, in part because of the tutoring, SES will become a legitimate and necessary part of public schooling, even if NCLB loses support. Then, he reasons, SES will be institutionalized and its value will go unquestioned just as private tutoring has become commonplace for children in middle- and upper-class families, aiming to get into top colleges.

United Education and other SES providers have their own measures of success (and failure). They don't include AYP goals, but focus instead on the quantity and quality of educational services and products they sell and deliver. Our bottom line is number of school accounts and dollars earned, explains the manager. Offering excellent SES programs and making money are not, he assures me, mutually exclusive. The better we do, the more we make. He pauses, and then admits that it is "theoretically possible that if we do our job too well, students won't need us, and we will have worked ourselves out of jobs." With more than two hundred thousand students eligible for SES in New York City this year, the possibility that a job too well done could be disastrous for United Education is not probable. The manager assures me that even with providers competing for market shares—i.e., student enrollments—there are enough "students in need" for all of the providers.

Scenario 4: Administrating from the Department of Education

I initially met the DOE administrator in 2005, when she had been a United Education manager. By the time I saw her listed as the "DOE contact" on an advertisement for a principals' workshop focusing on "data-driven instruction under NCLB" in March 2008, she had worked in the DOE's central office for a year. In electronic correspondence with the administrator, she admits that she now works on "the other side" of the public-private partnerships legislated through SES and acknowledges that she has great concerns about the lack of accountability attributed to the SES industry, for whom she once toiled. She resoundingly situates herself on the "side" of public education and is, after seeing what schools and districts must do under NCLB, against the mandated intervention of private tutoring companies.

According to the administrator, implementing NCLB continues to be challenging at the district level because people don't automatically do what they're told. They interpret what they are told to do before determining their responses. In the case of implementing NCLB, especially the SES mandates, the DOE and city officials are still trying to orient what they do to meet the federal rules, she reasons. The administrator notes that principals and schools plan actions according to the rules, but they are also trying to do what they interpret as best for their students. Since the two are not always the same, she admits that some principals have begun to "improvise implementation" and have begun "cutting SES corners."

The administrator doesn't fault the behavior of the principals, but rather blames NCLB itself, which she says impacts New York City, the country's largest school district, more than smaller, less urban districts with less diverse student populations. She explains that the city's public schools are filled with poor and minority students and that there are also many ELLs. These subpopulations, in NCLB terms, become AYP demographic groups, each with performance targets that must be met. The administrator adds that most of the SES programs do little, with regard to instruction and curricula, to attend to these subgroups.

Introduction

NCLB calls together many multifaceted actors in disparate organizations—like the ones depicted in the above scenarios—who bring different motivations, understandings, objectives, histories, and resources to the implementation of the mandates. *Making Failure Pay* is a book about what happens to NCLB, school failure, the substantive concern of the policy, and the additional problems it poses when these actors, and many others, respond and enact the federal policy locally. It is an investigation into how NCLB creates circumstances that limit the range of possible reactions and outcomes to school failure—and also how NCLB enables the creative and practical management of problems constituted by the uncertainties of the policy (Ball 2006). It is also a book about the struggles concerning enactment and interpretation of NCLB by actors, similar to the ones introduced in the opening situations, about the challenges in attending to school failure, and about the remarkable variation of responses to NCLB across contexts. As NCLB flows through federal, state, and local educational settings, and across a range of political and power configurations, the complexly situated actors selectively adapt or "appropriate" (Levinson and Sutton 2001) the policy mandates. A mix of intended and unintended consequences result (Datnow 2006) as these policy stakeholders, in and out of schools, apply particular elements of the policy to their situations.

Specifically, this book is about appropriating NCLB's SES, across state and local educational agencies, schools, and multiple educational support businesses.[5] It is about the interactional, and often unsteady, everyday NCLB-guided practices that move people, objects, and programs around school failure. This book illustrates that NCLB, which is federally mandated, state-regulated, district-administered, and school-applied, is a process that impacts American schooling, in part, by connecting the actions of numerous agents in multiple institutions—like testing and tutoring companies—which are associated with schools but have rarely been recognized for their increasingly integral roles in public education.

By mandating failing schools to contract with private tutoring companies to provide afterschool tutoring, SES blurs the boundaries between government, schooling, and commerce and brings the associations between public and private entities to the fore. SES explicitly expands the role of the private sector in public education, in governing educational bodies, and in schools. Under SES regulations, schools and their SES-eligible students become the "consumers" over which commercial marketers and enterprises compete. SES legitimizes tutoring by promoting the packaging, marketing, and selling of tutoring programs as commodities (complete with curricula and practices) that are then inserted into a dynamic network of relations, processes, and exchanges that traverse public organizations and private agencies.

SES encompasses the embedded authority, politics, potentials, and character of NCLB. Many of the struggles, contradictions, tensions, and interpretations of NCLB are made visible through SES, which must be implemented within particular localities, most often individual schools. Yet, the ways in which SES provisions stimulate and channel actions through levels of governmental organization, educational agencies, and emerging social structures have been largely unstudied. *Making Failure Pay* fills this lacuna by closely examining the interactions between a well-established for-profit SES provider, United Education,[6] and forty-two of its New York City partner schools. It reveals that attending to—defining, regulating, evaluating, and remedying—school failure, according to NCLB, provokes a host of inadvertent, conspicuous, and abtruse consequences, or problems, not the least of which is more failure.

Ethnographic Considerations for Studying Everyday Policy Processes

Making Failure Pay documents the appropriation of NCLB by tracing the linkages between the New York City school district, public schools across five boroughs, city government, and United Education. Integrating the federal and state actions with the more localized interactions, it traces "policy connections between different organizational and everyday worlds, even where actors in different sites do not know each other or share a moral universe" (Shore and Wright 1997, 14). This book demands a shift in the analytical focus from students and teachers to situations that occur outside of classroom instruction and beyond official school hours, in public settings and at publicized events that are infused with the authority of the federal and state education departments. This ethnography moves well beyond schools to consider the ways in which failure is made to matter in policy, in private educational companies, in politics, in local and state educational agencies, in schools, and in American culture. Based on more than three years of ethnographic research, conducted from June 2005 to October 2008, it examines what happens to school failure and the federal remedy, NCLB, when people—adults in the public school system, the tutoring and testing industry, and the policy-making institutions—engage in policy-directed activities, especially SES.

This book challenges conventional educational ethnography and educational policy analysis in three important ways. First, it reduces the gap between everyday actions and activities and government action. Second, *Making Failure Pay* concurrently regards the actions of disparate policy stakeholders, including SES managers and politicians who foray temporarily into policy processes, and principals whose policy roles persist, often over years. Third, it expands the field of study to transactional spaces that transcend physical locations. Further, this book considers the historical consciousness of the participants and documents the historical development of NCLB and SES, while studying actors in present moments. This book progresses from a strictly synchronic ethnographic frame to a "historicization of the ethnographic present" (Marcus and Fischer 1999, 95–97).

This unconventional approach to the ethnographic study of policy results in an original view of NCLB's almost invisible, costly, and risky public-private liaisons that transfer federal education funding to companies that profit by providing unproven and unregulated afterschool tutoring. The merit of this book's perspective, however, extends beyond an innovative analysis of NCLB-created situations to the broader consideration of various "federal sanctions–driven approaches" (Mintrop and Sunderman 2009) enacted across wide-ranging entities. Whether it be Goals 2000, No Child Left Behind, Race to the Top (an educational component of the $787 billion American Recovery and Reinvestment Act), or a future set of rules on how a polity must conduct itself concerning matters of public education, different groups of policy stakeholders, under varying rubrics of accountability and sanction, will be brought together to appropriate it locally across varied terrains. NCLB, as situated in this book, represents but one strand of a complexly related web of educational policies, practices, and politics—and as argued here, these policies are, and will be texturally, practically, and discursively contingent and historically interrelated in ways that warrant multileveled investigation.

Studying "up" (Nader 1974), studying "vertically" (Vavrus and Bartlett 2009), and "studying through" (Reinhold 1994) policy situations as I have done in this book requires innovative methodology, including constructing a composite company, United Education. Utilizing the composite is likely, I acknowledge, to give readers pause and to evoke questions about what might have been compromised by its creation. I recognize that presenting United Education as a hybrid entity renders the reproduction of my study difficult. From the beginning of my research to the writing of this book, I wrestled with presenting data in ways that maintain the credibility and reliability of the data, while protecting the identity and positions of all the participants. Ultimately, I concluded, as I hope my readers do, that the composite strengthens the study, allowing me to best illuminate the complexities, contradictions, and fluidity of associations as heterogeneous policy elements are assembled and reassembled by various actors, like those presented in the four scenarios.

Using a composite is rare in educational ethnographies. The technique is, in fact, nearly unprecedented in the anthropological and sociological scholarship on education. In "The Horace Trilogy," a set of "non-fiction fiction" books, Sizer (1984, 1992, and 1997) creates Horace, who is a composite character drawn from observations of "scores of teachers and schools" (1984, xi) to which the author attributes patterns of behaviors. In contrast, United Education, the composite SES provider in this book, is assembled from separately verifiable and public facts about five similarly organized and managed for-profit tutoring companies. I have not ascribed patterns of activities to the composite, but have attributed only situations, actions, and circumstances that were well documented, either through observational field notes, written (mostly public) documents, or interviews.[7]

The composite functions similarly to the more commonly used pseudonym. Schools (or organizations) represented by ethnographic pseudonyms are not meant to be identified or "found," but they are believed to be geographically fixed and, thus, locatable. Many associated with a study or linked tangentially to it—the participants and the ethnographer's colleagues, for instance—often in fact, know the actual school. Nonetheless, pseudonyms are used to provide some sense of confidentiality for study participants. Consider that in New York City, during the time of this study, there were between 1,400 and 1,500 schools, and it would have been possible to "conceal" the identity of a researched school and most certainly the identities of those in the school using pseudonyms; at the same time, less than one hundred SES providers were actively providing services, and of the hundred, less than twenty enjoyed the vast majority of SES contracts. The five companies from which I constructed United hail from those twenty providers. Presenting the data from only one of these companies, even under pseudonym, would have drastically increased the possibility of recognition.

Later in this chapter, I provide a descriptive image of United Education by integrating the specific descriptions of each company. The five companies from which United is drawn are similar in their bureaucratic organization, their SES programs, their missions, and the quantity of school accounts and students enrolled. Four existed as educational support companies prior to NCLB, and one was started during 2002. So similar are the actions taken by the five companies in response to NCLB that public records and government reports often aggregate them, along with other providers, under the rubric of "well-known" or "well-established" SES providers. Any numbers and statistics I attribute to United are averaged without distorting the overall services or programs of each component company. Admittedly, however, what is lost by using the composite is an analysis of interactions *between* providers. Yet, all of this is necessary to protect study participants, to meet my responsibility to my discipline of anthropology, and to be responsive to those involved in policy processes.[8]

Approaching Educational Policy and School Failure

Making Failure Pay takes as its beginning a profound suspicion that failure is not what it seems, that policy is much more that it appears. It elucidates the linkages between policy and school failure as part of "the social," in which uncertainty and arbitrariness abound in cultural circumstances replete with emerging constraints and structures.[9] Policy is observed as a complex process that involves the situated actions of many across varied contexts and failure is not an intact identifiable "thing" as much as it is a shared social and cultural achievement of localized practices. Policy is set forth and put into practice in "a field or a network of relations constantly subject to the play of power, both within and from without, and beset by struggles for positional advantage" (Ball 2006, 3), and the potential of each policy-activated agent is locally realized and personally communicated.

This book is firmly situated within the ethnographic study of policy—integrating "policy sociology" (Ozga 1987; Ball 2006), "anthropology of policy" (Shore and Wright 1997), and "policy as practice" (Levinson and Sutton 2001)—which compels us to distinguish and study policy as the ongoing human activities through which it is made to fit particular situations. It is also linked with what Willis and Trondman (2000) have coined "*procedural* policy work," in their words, the utilization of "theoretically informed ethnographies to expand the resources of knowledge and information which social actors use to understand their own position and the likely consequences of particular courses of action, so absorbing concepts and theories *about* them *into* their actual practice" (11, emphasis in original). Recognizing policy as processes draws attention to the negotiated interactions, iterations, and enactions through which NCLB is articulated. It resituates what we have come to know and accept about NCLB by emphasizing how the policy, the actions it prescribes, the actors who become involved, and the fluctuating definition of the circumstances mutually shape school failure.

Applying actor-network theory (Latour 1995, 2005) to the study of policy establishes a methodologically rigorous means by which to study the ways in which agents across multiple and various organizations and agencies link together—associate or assemble—to simultaneously appropriate NCLB and make sense of the situations afforded by the policy's mandates.[10] The theory provides a way in which "to grasp the interactions (and disjunctions) between different sites or levels in policy processes" (Shore and Wright 1997, 14) and to follow the "continuous connections leading from one local interaction to the other places, times, and agencies" (Latour 2005, 173). As actors in federal government, state educational agencies, local educational agencies, and the educational support industry converge under the mandates of NCLB, they act together, sharing knowledge, expanding their connections, and mediating future actions. They engage in contextualization, they analyze and interpret their somewhat shared situation, and they organize their attention to school failure by drawing on the contexts in which they must adapt NCLB.

Attending to failure demands the mobilization of rules and resources through ongoing processes of mediation, which are endlessly negotiated, highly multifaceted, and only somewhat disciplined. The actions of many are a "continuous flow of conduct" (Giddens 1979, 5) that could at any time have been done otherwise. The practical actions are taken for everyday purposes (Garfinkel 1967) and are the result of the temporary associations between schools, government, and commerce that organize the "practices of everyday life" (11). Actors in these associations actively construct their activities, making sense of their own actions and legitimizing their interpretations of NCLB. Taylor and Van Every (2000) remind us that the immediate task of "sensemaking" occurs first at some individual level and then second as shared local interaction among actors who act together on a regular basis (147). In this book, actors improvise their roles over time, performing them in order to create some sensibility.

Nonhuman objects, like NCLB, can be mobilized by human actors. Once linked to human actors, such nonhuman objects, which are often denied in cultural analysis, become an admittedly important part of culture. In fact, they join with human agents to create joint vectors of agency, and together, they do things. They mediate, they translate, and they get other entities to take action. NCLB enters schools as a script, a written directive for what should happen in failing schools, and, through the actions of many, the local implementation of NCLB becomes a set of transcripts, accounts of what actually happens when actors act.[11] To act—to make a difference (Giddens 1984, 14)—is to mobilize one or more objects and perhaps other human actors to construct environments and attend to the daily situations of attending to school failure. Once mobilized, nonhuman actors can continue to act in the absence of the original subject partner, thus becoming part of the network that extends beyond any single interaction.

Methodologically employing actor-network theory hinges upon following "the actors' own ways" by starting with "the traces left behind by their activity and forming and dismantling groups" (Latour 2005, 29). One of the main actors, NCLB, is cast as the latest set of rules in an ongoing cultural construction of public schooling and school failure in America, rather than as a radical shift in thinking and action. Actions mandated by NCLB have deep ancestry in the culturing and commercialization of schooling, in which meritocracy, accountability, standardization, and centralization have endured as key components. *Making Failure Pay* reveals that policy's SES regulations are sated not with directives to strengthen schools, but rather with authorizations to radically centralize state powers, increase the privatization of services, standardize local activities, and further categorize children as failing. NCLB, we will begin to see in the next chapter, is not a "necessarily legitimate representation of 'public' needs and interests" (Levinson and Sutton 2001, 2) but instead a persuasive textual product and a powerful sociocultural process that guides adults to collude in taking actions that make failure matter.

The study's findings indicate that what is significant is not dependent on actors as personalized identities, but as members of a network to which people are accountable to, directly and indirectly, at the time of the interaction. To emphasize this finding and to draw attention to all the actors and all their actions, I choose to use generic position titles, such as "principal" and "manager" rather than personalize the pseudonyms. The findings also point to the increased theoretical and methodological potency of utilizing actor-network theory (Latour 1995, 2005) to extend the analysis beyond face-to-face human interactions, however contextualized, to an ever-changing multileveled and positioned network of actors, relationships, and actions. Unlike other explanations of school failure that attempt to reconcile the local situation of failure with global frames, this book focuses on the sociocultural—the interactions, associations, and relations along which actors at remedying school failure flow and through which actors make their behaviors accountable in their everyday work situations.

No Child Left Behind

According to the NCLB legislation, all public school children should be the focus of educational efforts. However, as shown throughout this book, some children are left out, or at least left behind, in NCLB, the very legislation that mandates such a thing should be impossible. According to its executive summary, NCLB intends to "improve the performance of America's elementary and secondary schools while at the same time ensuring that *no* child is trapped in a failing school" (U.S. Department of Education 2001), but scholars (Darling-Hammond 2004; Wood 2004) explain that the NCLB Act will, in the next few years, label most of the nation's public schools as failing. Even the Act's basic goal of attaining 100 percent proficiency levels for students on tests, where some must score below any determined success-failure divide, creates a fundamental dilemma and a mathematical impossibility that excludes children who are hard at work, "doing" school.

Since its passage in 2002, NCLB has become central to the organization of America's educational system. As both policy and law, its normative power lays partly in its unobjectionable agenda—to provide the highest quality education for "all" children in fourteen thousand school districts across fifty states, the District of Columbia, and Puerto Rico. Providing the nation's schools with the universal and desirable, if unattainable, goal of preventing all children from school failure, NCLB offers a common-sense solution. Few, if any, would argue that some children should be purposefully left behind. The name, in fact, disguises the disparities and inconsistencies of the policy while reassuring the public of its common good (Edelman 1985). Camouflaged in persuasive wording and costumed as the final solution to school failure, NCLB seems to be an objective and neutral cultural tool.

Implementing NCLB locally results in a series of actions by and connections between diverse actors across various social and institutional contexts. It requires that large-scale "collectives" or "organizations" are forged. At the beginning of this study, there are diverse actors, each with their own resources, histories, and intentions. They are engaged in their everyday work; teachers are teaching, administrators are administering, and officials are governing. Then, NCLB is positioned as a common solution to the problem of failure by the federal government. The actors begin to associate with each other and form linkages when confronted by

NCLB, which directs them all to attend to school failure. After a period of "problematization," where actors' awareness of the problem is heightened, the actors identify their interest in one of the policy's mandates, providing SES. The state and local educational agencies recognize that they must set up a system for SES programs in failing schools. Principals of failing schools discern that they must invite SES providers into their schools to offer afterschool programs. Companies that provide SES become determined to persuade schools to enter into contract with them. And so on. A differentiated aligning of roles begins to emerge; actors mobilize, form associations, and construct their environments. The actors have been translated into an "actor-network" (Callon and Latour 1981; Latour 2005), complete with convoluted, contradictory, and conflicting associations.

United Education

United Education is a national for-profit, educational support company and provider of SES. United Education has hundreds of employees in a number of states across the United States and currently offers a range of educational services for individual students and schools, including curriculum and professional development for teachers and afterschool tutoring and academic instruction. According to members of United's executive administrators, United is an organization that focuses on quality and results; it is a company that has built its reputation on providing high-quality educational services and products. United continues to expand its educational programs, but, according to the company's president, it remains "true to its original values of being student-focused and results-driven." United is built upon a commitment to excellence of services and products. A company vice president confirms that United is "absolutely committed to our students' success . . . to ensure that they have every opportunity to learn in a way that suits them" (letter to New York City regional superintendents dated October 4, 2005).

Casting their programs and services as unique and "custom-designed to meet a district's or a school's specific needs," United partners with several urban school districts, including New York City. According to their marketing materials, United provides solutions that "provide school districts with the capacity and expertise to support a variety of initiatives, including No Child Left Behind" and "enable educators to provide ongoing, formative benchmark tests, with results reported at the district, school, class, and student levels" (Partnering with Schools Brochure 2006).

When principals were asked why they chose to buy products, such as curricula, and services, such as SES programs from United, they echoed a version of the company's message—because we want high-quality, proven materials that are tailored to students' learning styles. The principal of Public School (PS) 100 in Brooklyn similarly remarked of United's SES program: "We want to partner with United because United is a professional company that focuses on delivering good education by using well-trained instructors" (interview, October 17, 2007). A parent coordinator in Staten Island noted that her school chose United's SES because other schools in the area were pleased with the program's results.

The message that United's products and services "help students succeed in big ways" was also reiterated by employees (United employee, interview, January 18, 2007). Overall, staff members say that they believe in the products and services provided by the company. Many note that the company's focus on helping the children that need extra instruction resonates with the federal aims of NCLB. Two-thirds of those interviewed stated that their work and the work of United Education influenced the success of students throughout New York City.

United's SES programs in New York City were labor and cost intensive, but remained profitable by securing contracts with large schools and offsetting costs with its use of part-time seasonal employees. During this study, there were less than one dozen full-time SES employees, but more than two hundred active part-time staff—namely, supervisors and instructors—who worked onsite at schools during the afterschool programs. Full-time managers supervised part-time workers; other full-time support staff were responsible for generating and managing all the necessary program documentation including enrollment forms; student rosters; student attendance; teacher attendance; processing pre-, mid-, and post-program test results; and parent-guardian correspondence. Marketing United's SES program to schools and securing school accounts were responsibilities shared by all full-time SES employees and select part-time field staff.[12] Many positions overlapped, and the workloads fluctuated with the academic calendar as different employees assumed multiple responsibilities at various times of the year.

Once partnerships with schools were established and the details of the program set, United focused on staffing the programs with instructors, marketing SES to parents, and enrolling students. At schools, part-time teaching staff were recruited, hired, and trained. Curriculum, published by United, and other teaching materials, like pencils and notebooks, were ordered and delivered. In the office, a variety of databases for attendance, material tracking, and employee performance were created, and data was entered. So, many actions were taken to produce materials, including, but certainly not limited to, attendance records, student rosters, notifications to parents, emergency forms, time sheets, and identification cards, that would keep United in compliance with the redundant and variably enforced SES regulations established at the level of the state and district in accordance with NCLB.

The State, the Department of Education, and the Schools

Across the country, NCLB increases the demands on state and district agencies, as well as schools. The responsibility for implementing NCLB, like other federal policies, falls mostly to the states. However, because centers of organization and governance are broadly dispersed throughout states—and because New York City, the largest school district in the country, has a strong central authority—the city's DOE enjoyed an increased capacity to determine the implementation of NCLB during this study. When the research began, the DOE had an entire office, complete with rules and sanctions, devoted to administering SES according to the federal and state regulations. In turn, school principals, who were among the 259 SINI schools mandated, in 2005–6, to provide SES, had appointed an "SES contact person," usually an assistant principal or parent coordinator to organize the SES and develop relationships with SES providers. By the end of the study, nearly 340 of the city's schools were offering SES and the student participation rate, in 2005–8, was, at nearly 12 percent. Still, many children (between thirty and thirty-five thousand per year) did not complete the SES programs after enrolling, and state and city officials, as well as tutoring company executives, blamed each other for the lack of program completion.

Localizing NCLB's tutoring mandates in the city was intertwined within the mayor's and schools chancellor's implementation of sweeping Children First standard-based reforms and a complete reorganization of the city's education structure. The reforms and their intersections with NCLB appropriation, which are discussed at length in chapter 2, reveal that policy appropriation is political and illustrate that policy "stakeholders do not have the same access to power in the process of implementation" (Dumas and Anyon 2006, 165). In New York City, the mayor, with absolute control of the DOE, set about renovating what he considered a multiplicity of academic, operational, and structural weaknesses in the schooling system, which encompassed the district's 1,400 schools and 1.1 million students.

Educational Policy in Multiple Contexts

NCLB is an authoritative declaration of purposeful action. Instrumentally, it focuses on the association between directives and outcomes and is used to regulate and organize behavior (Stein 2004). It allocates values—benefits, responsibilities, and burdens—to policy actors. NCLB, in this sense, presupposes that actions directed at remedying school failure, including SES, can be comprehensively planned and nationally legislated (Smith 2004). It defines the situation of school failure and generates rules and norms by which actors should behave. Nonetheless, while NCLB creates circumstances and situations that narrow or change the possible actions, responses to the policy "must still be put together, constructed in context, off-set against or balanced by other expectations" (Ball 2006, 21). The policy guides, but does not determine, actions directed at school failure. According to Elmore and McLaughlin (1982), federal policies, like NCLB, "are prescriptions about what ought to be done, but they are also conditional statements that contain some degree of uncertainty about the causal relationship between government action and the results it is intended to produce" (173). Creative and practical responses, such as those hinted at by the DOE administrator in scenario 4, are required of actors who are responsible for implementing NCLB.

NCLB is best conceptualized and studied as a productive social practice. Levinson and Sutton (2001) suggest that policy is "an ongoing process of normative cultural production constituted by diverse actors across diverse social and institutional contexts" (1). As it becomes articulated, NCLB is "both contested and changing, always in a state of becoming, of was and never was and not quite" (Ball 2006, 44). It is open to multiple and repeated interpretations by key interlocutors, such as the principal of MS 200 in the second scenario, the SES manager in the third, and the DOE administrator in the fourth. NCLB is carried out by many such policy participants, working across a "large loosely jointed governance system"

(Fuhrman 1993, 42), a fragmented educational authority, and weakly linked private agencies. As the federal government aims to direct the actions of state and local educational agencies, through NCLB, those who ultimately apply policy significantly mediate implementation through their participation in collective sense making (Honig 2006b). Thus, the policy becomes encoded with struggles, compromises, and alternative interpretations and is decoded via actors' interpretations, experiences, and resources.

Just as the actors in this study adjust to NCLB, the policy shifts to the contexts in which it is enacted. Contexts in which policy is "done" are inextricable from the policy itself (Dumas and Anyon 2006, 151); actors' policy-informed actions are shaped by the situations and settings in which they are executed (Datnow, Hubbard, and Mehan 2002). NCLB, however sweeping in its scope, does not operate in isolation. It is influenced by the locations in which it is situated and the interactions with multiple federal, state, and district-based educational policies. The SES manager turned DOE administrator points to the inordinate burden NCLB places on large urban school districts, such as New York City's. The principal of MS 200 speaks of the intersections between the federal and local policies, which are "simultaneously in motion, with one inhibiting or prohibiting the actions required by the enactment of another" (Ball 2006, 17).

In New York City, NCLB interacts with "Children First: A New Agenda for Public Education in New York City" (Children First), the market-based reforms aimed at increasing accountability for individual schools and principals. The interchange between NCLB and Children First, mentioned by the MS 200 principal and documented in later chapters, results in combined emphasis on peformativity of individuals, schools, districts, and states—and an accountability based on standardized measures of evaluation and comparisons. Monitoring, documenting, and rewarding achievement valued by these policies demand increasingly sophisticated databases, reviews, and reports—which in turn contribute to the increased weight of school failure, especially for school principals like the one in the second scenario.

NCLB is open to the fluctuations in political and programmatic responses to school failure, to the very phenomena at which it is aimed. Failure gets reified as it circulates through institutional contexts and is identified, interpreted, amplified, remedied, and sometimes challenged by a multiplicity of agents. Variable local constructions—complete with consensus and contestation—of school failure are generated as actors make sense of their ceaselessly changing circumstances and bring "order" to the chaotic situations constructed when a country is legislated to localize and enact NCLB. School principals, elected educational officials, tutoring industry managers, and many others, not only cope with what comes their way because of the policy, but actually reorganize their daily responses to failure.

As NCLB is produced, interpreted, reconceptualized, and interwoven into multiple policy-informed practices, interpretations of failure, and measurable outcomes, it poses problems that are grappled with and worked out in context, through localized actions. In particular, enacting the SES mandates within a paradoxical situation—a competitive free market and centralization of educational authority—brings into relation actors from public schools, government, and for-profit educational business with different ideologies, accountabilities, and commitments. As illustrated throughout this book, the relationships between these entities are temporary and often tenuous, as the various actors interpret and respond to the situations afforded them by the policy mandates. As these actors conduct their everyday work, in schools, in government, and in the tutoring industry, they accomplish real tasks, institute regular practices, and establish their NCLB-directed authority.

Often, however, as examined in the following chapters, the actions and activities initiated in response to the NCLB and SES directives are discordant, contradictory, and competitive. When actors are legislated to systematically turn their attentions to school failure, a host of substantial logistical, financial, practical, and ethical concerns and problems are generated. Because policy-guided activities are not context free, they are constrained and enabled differentially by the settings in which they are prescribed to occur (Scott 2008). Consequential dilemmas are created when many people attend urgently to school failure; troubles arise when failure, or the signs of failure, are neglected; and a cascade of problems prevail when failure is invented or fabricated—all according to multiple constructions, interpretations, and understandings of NCLB.

Organization of the Study

In the following chapter, I expand the discussion of policy studies and policy theory begun in this introductory chapter. Theory is necessary, I argue, as it "provides a possibility of a difference language, a language which is not caught up with the assumptions and inscriptions of policy-makers or the immediacy of practice" (Ball 2006, 20). Actor-network theory, which is explored in the second half of the chapter, shows how this ethnography captures the multiplicity of NCLB beyond limiting the analytic possibilities of overarching contexts, structures, or forces to re-veal many participants simultaneously working on interactions that over-flow in all directions (Latour 2005).

In chapter 3, I examine the associations between schools and SES pro-viders. I show that while the SES industry is highly constrained in proce-dural directions—where students must sign in, how attendance is submit-ted, etc.—it is not exactly regulated, not exactly proven, and not exactly funded. More important, in contrast to their school partners, SES providers are minimally accountable for student participation and test outcomes. Still, enrolling students in a competitive open market equals receipt of Title I funds for providers. Many principals, however, are hesitant, if not resistant, to reallocate the funds to SES. Some explicitly discourage student participation. Such conflicts have led to a variety of questionable actions by SES providers, including misappropriation and misuse of confidential student information, the failure to conduct background and fingerprint checks on instructors, improper parental solicitation, offers of money to school employees in exchange for enrolled students, monetary donations to schools, and the offering of self-serving incentive programs—including CD players, tickets to sporting events, and gift cards. Tenuous relation-ships between schools and SES providers have also stimulated actions by principals that seem not to attend to failing students.

In chapters 4 through 6, my attention turns to the distinct ways the SES provider–school partnerships make failure matter in the American social milieu. I examine variable local constructions—complete with consensus and contestation—of school failure. Connecting microprocesses such as an SES instructor–principal interaction with macroprocesses of educa-tion such as the redistribution of Children First funds in New York City's Title I schools demonstrates that failure gets reified by a mutliplicity of agents as it circulates through institutional contexts. The cases presented in the three chapters illustrate the ways in which actors make sense of their ceaselessly changing circumstances and bring "order" to the chaotic situations constructed when a country is legislated to localize and follow a plan of action for attending to school failure. School principals, elected educational officials, tutoring industry managers, and many others not only cope with what comes their way, but actually reconstruct their situations through their actions and activities.

Attending to school failure as prescribed by NCLB requires that timely actions be taken. In chapter 4, I document the urgency by some schools and SES providers to address failure results in unanticipated responses. Interactions between the school's principal, assistant principal, and parent coordinator—all of whom expected United to be the school's "lifeline"—and the United field manager, who was given the ominous task to "save the school" in sixty program hours, are examined. The school administrators cast the school's failure as extraordinary when NCLB measures showed otherwise. This resulted in two undesirable consequences for the principal. First, fifty-three parents, citing the excessive focus on testing, tutoring, and other academic interventions, requested that their children be transferred to other schools. Second, after a series of meetings, United decided not to renew their contract with the school the following year, noting that the school's overemphasis on failure made their job impossible.

The two other examples presented in chapter 4 focus on how the call to urgently direct attention to school failure manifests outside schools. The first focuses on how the urgency to "fix" schools gets transformed, literally translated, into an urgency to get a larger share of the tutoring market during various United staff meetings. In the second instance, the ratification of the United Federation of Teachers contract in 2007, which added 37.5 minutes of small-group instruction for failing students, required even more urgent action by parents, school staff, allied staff (including bus drivers, security guards, and food service employees), and afterschool SES providers. Both examples illustrate how many people attending to and constructing the urgent need to attend to school failure created consequential problems.

Chapter 5 offers another perspective to making failure matter—by neglecting it. The first case explores the actions taken by a Brooklyn elementary school when its contract with United Education conflicted with its commitments to Great Works, a community-based organization housed within the school. The need to partner with an SES provider set the administration of PS 472 into a series of actions and inactions that led to a myriad of problems for themselves, Great Works, United Education, and the children, who ultimately did not receive academic support in a safe and stable environment. After the principal declined to provide adequate rooms for United's program and refused to pull students out of the Great

Works activities in order to attend SES two days a week, United, for the only time in its history, petitioned the DOE to remove its SES program from the school, leaving the students without an SES provider.

In the second example in the chapter, United Education neglected the failing test scores of prospective instructors and hired them despite their inability to answer half of the questions correctly on an eighth-grade level mathematics examination. Given during the last hour of a twelve-hour training course as an evaluative test disguised as a normative one, the exams were intended to eliminate candidates from employment. However, from one training class, six of the eleven instructors who failed the examination were scheduled the following week to teach seventh- and eighth-grade SES classes.

Chapter 6 illustrates multiple inventions of failure. Making failure matter requires a mocking-up or an exaggeration of failure and/or a misinterpretation, intentional or otherwise, of the signs of failure. It also demands, more often than we may realize, the fabrication of failure—the performing of failure, where none of the accepted markers by which we have come to recognize and name it actually exists. In the three cases illustrated in this chapter, the school staff and their partner SES provider, United Education, invent failure through their activities.

In the chapter's first example, which is set at a Queens' junior high school, a United instructor repeatedly drilled students on the multiplication tables, for which they had already demonstrated proficiency. Through her actions, the instructor deemed the students to be failures, requiring remediation; in turn, her students co-constructed her as a failing teacher who was unable to teach anything beyond basic math skills, like multiplication tables. Compounding these constructions of failure, the United staff and the school's principal chose not to use United test results diagnostically. Each noted that NCLB only required that tests be administered and that the scores made available to the school and to the students' parents. It did not necessitate adjusting curriculum or teaching according to tests results, which according to United was beyond the scope of their responsibilities and capacities in their afterschool programs. Administering the practice tests took precedence over using the results to target students' areas of weakness. Both United and the junior high school staff were, indeed, attending to school failure by performing the actions that were recognized, mostly by the parents, as those needed to attend to failure.

The second case begins with a United supervisor manufacturing low scores on students' SES pretest scores at a Staten Island elementary school, PS 80. Fearing that students' actual pretest scores of 80 percent or more would make it impossible for the SES program to show improvement, he manipulated the test scores with the hopes that the posttests would show dramatic improvement, and thus place United in a favorable position to be invited back to the school the following year. As his actions became known to United's senior management staff, steps to explain, if not cover-up, the falsified failing scores to parents and the school's principal ensued.

In the final instance, nearly everyone at PS 100 in Brooklyn and United Education also addressed the problem of failure. What makes this remarkable is that PS 100 was not failing. PS 100 is a barrier-free school that mainstreams special education students and ELLs in regular classes; the DOE's failure to include the scores of these particular subsets of PS 100 students in the calculations resulted in their designation. Mistakenly placed on the SINI list, the school staff and the parents, nonetheless, developed ways to address the failure. PS 100 was a New York City "failing school" that was not failing and as the staffs of United and the school tried to make sense of this designation, failure overshadowed the school's actual success. That failure was made to matter at all in this case shows that we do not need failing students or failing groups of students to make failure matter.

In the final chapter, I reassemble the fragments of the network by focusing on the flow of work to summarize the book's findings. I begin with NCLB, which is, in fact, somewhat of a middle, *in media res,* of the network. I show how the authority of NCLB was carried out by many interlocutors in multiple interactions. In contrast to established theories of social organization that present social collectives as a structured entity—a hierarchy of offices, productive process, and work (e.g., organizational flow chart)—I make clear that the organization of the network was continually "becoming" and constantly evolving; the potential of each agent was being locally realized and personally communicated.

I conclude not with a solution to the problem that has come to be known and performed as school failure, but rather with suggestions about how educational researchers might subvert the commonsense notions of failure (McDermott and Varenne 2006, 23). I confront the conditions that have historically linked and continue to join school failure with all the ineffectual solutions. I ask that educational anthropologists not only

question our subjectivity as researchers, but also acknowledge our participation as cultural members who contribute to the conditions by becoming part of the NCLB network when we study the policy. Yet, of course,
we are not only researchers look in at schooling from the outside. We are
students and teachers and community activists and parents of schoolchildren; we are, in my understanding, policy makers.

Drawing on the book's examples, I suggest the ways in which this ethnography alone can inform policy decisions. NCLB may or may not be
reauthorized, but there will be no shortage of federal educational policies
with which to contend. I advocate for ways in which we, as educational
researchers, might enter into dialogues of school reform and educational
policy analysis that move beyond description and evaluation—that provide some possibilities for different kinds of actions. I also ask that we
continue to find new strategies by which to demonstrate that failure does
not, indeed, matter so very much. In sum, I ask that we do our part to
make our work matter much more, and in doing so, make failure matter
much less.

FRAMING FAILURE

Interrogating Policy Studies, Policy Theory, and NCLB

To date, the Elementary and Secondary Education Act (ESEA) of 1965, reauthorized for the eighth time in 2002 as the No Child Left Behind (NCLB) Act, stands as the main federal policy aimed specifically at narrowing the achievement gap in Title I schools in America's fifty states, Puerto Rico, and the District of Columbia.[1] NCLB seeks to close "the achievement gap between high and low-performing children, especially the achievement gaps between minority and non-minority students, and between disadvantaged children and their more advantaged peers" (NCLB 2001, Sec. 1001 [3]). Title I of the Act provides money to state education agencies to implement the federal policy through designing programs to "upgrade the education of deprived children" (Sizer 2004, xx).[2] However, Title I, the largest compensatory federal education program aimed at school failure, has resulted in a fractured network of disparate programs and accountability measures that satisfy the federal government's obligation to track spending rather than attending to the educational needs of children (Stein 2004).

NCLB persists in the social construction (and social judgments) of "disadvantaged" children, the policy's target population, and furthers a particular presentation of the popular and enduring "faith in using schools as a lever of social progress" (Reese 2005, 322) for those categorized as most needy—i.e., poor minority children. In their critical social analysis of educational policy, Dumas and Anyon (2006) make clear that "class and race are intrinsically connected social constructs" (166) and that the policy references to the "urban poor" are intended to connote "colored faces" (167). Casting the problem as "individual attributes and behaviors, rather than on structural or institutional conditions" (Stein 2004, xiii), NCLB represents the surface expression of deep histopolitical, sociocultural, and ideological discourses in American education that cast poor minority students as failing (and therefore deviant) and in need of government intervention. The "contention about the problem of the problem," McLaughlin (2006) notes, is "nowhere more prevalent than in education, where problem statements are often taken for granted, as commonplace notions" (210–11). As Edelman (1988) reminds us, "the language that constructs a problem and provides an origin for it is also a rationale for vesting authority in people who claim some kind of competence" (20). NCLB is made possible, if not probable, by nearly two centuries of culturing schooling in America, in which the low academic achievement of individuals and selected groups—most recently, poor and black children— have been made noteworthy, if not prominent. Undergirding the policy's 588 regulations is an emphasis on individual merit and strict accountability, enduring ideals in America that most burden those groups of students who have historically been depicted as low achieving.

Making and Remaking Policy

NCLB follows the historical implementation of ESEA, in which broad assistance objectives have been replaced by narrower compliance goals as the government prompts specific local responses instead of increasing and supporting local responsiveness (Elmore and McLaughlin 1982). Nonetheless, like other federal educational policies, NCLB is open to multiple improvisations, and local responses are anything but uniform. This dynamic nature of policy is explained by Levinson and Sutton (2001), who note that "policy serves at various levels of government as a legitimating charter for the techniques of administration and as an operational manual for everyday conduct; it is the symbolic expression of normative claims worked into a potentially viable institutional blueprint" (2). Although NCLB begins as a course or method of action, among many, selected by the federal government, given the perceived condition of school failure, there are multiple "collisions" between governmental intentions, policy directives, and educational practices (Fuhrman 1993, 42). As a set of stated principles, NCLB directs, but does not determine, the performance of activities enlisted across, and within, state and local levels to achieve certain goals, including leaving no child behind.

The development and implementation of NCLB is well described as the sociocultural "appropriation" of policy, which Levinson and Sutton (2001) define as "the way creative agents 'take in' elements of policy, thereby incorporating these discursive and institutional resources into their own schemes of interest, motivation, and action" (3). The appropriation of educational policy highlights the actions of local actors' interpretations and negotiations of such policy into the contexts of their everyday interactions and practices. By recasting "policy as a complex social practice, an ongoing process of normative cultural production constituted by diverse actors across diverse social and institutional contexts" (1), Levinson and Sutton resituate policy, the problem to which it attends, the practices it prescribes, the social actors who are to perform the practices, and the contexts in which the practices are performed.

The NCLB mandates are "real things" to which many must attend, but what NCLB accomplishes is diffuse and multidirectional as actors interpret and construct the policy for their own means. Agents appropriate the policy and construct their roles and actions in relation to the policy, to each other, and to existing power relations. In their co-"construction" theory of policy implementation, Datnow, Hubbard, and Mehan (2002) argue that the policy appropriation exhibits multidirectionality as actors in multiple levels of an educational system influence reform. Emphasizing a "relational sense of context," Datnow (2006, 107) notes that policy actions, as well as policy contexts, are influential in shaping policy implementation. NCLB is made, negotiated, resisted, unmade, and remade by the actions of many across multiple localized and politicized situations.

As demonstrated in recent studies (O'Day 2002; Hamann and Lane 2004; Anyon 2005), places and settings beyond schools, such as state and local educational agencies and private urban institutions, are also to be considered important policy contexts. Recent anthropological studies of

NCLB and related policies (Bartlettet al. 2002; Salinas 2007) have documented the linkages between the accountability in political and business contexts and the accountability policies adopted by national, state, and local educational entities. They argue that through specific discourses and actions, these accountability reforms gain purchase across political, commercial, and educational settings. Coburn (2005), in her study of "nonsystem" actors' roles in the educational policy processes, notes that a plethora of actors outside of schools "promote, translate, and even transform policy ideas" (23). She argues that these actors, whom she identifies as "independent professional development providers, reform organizations, publishers, and universities [and, I would add, education researchers]," mediate between policy and practice, ultimately influencing teachers' actions, through the policy messages imbued through their intense, long-standing, and often voluntary interactions with the teachers.

Commercializing and Politicizing Policy

As NCLB is localized, it is nearly immediately "followed by many other statements that further specify what it is to entail" (Varenne 2007, 17). NCLB, as we now speak of it, represents a loud culminating (and summarizing) voice, responding in the moment to "a temporal sequence that includes all sorts of other utterances performed by any number of institutional agents" (17). Most of the people who are required to take action under NCLB have never read the original policy; they have relied on subsequently generated verbal and written distillations of the policy. In this way, NCLB works "as discourse" (Ball 1993; 1994)—the practices by which a policy "exercises power through a production of 'truth' and 'knowledge' as discourses" (Ball 2006, 48). It is imparted with a variety of discourses—some complimentary and others discordant—that repositions what is said by some actors, often of the state, as more authoritative, powerful, or "truthful."

NCLB is continually constructed through the flow of diffused actions across many situations and relations permeated with power; however, the authority of NCLB to politically regulate the efficiency of a schooling system that operates on multilateral legislative and organizational levels cannot be overlooked. Because "power is multiplicitous, overlain, interactive and complex, policy texts enter rather than simply change power relations" (Ball 2006, 46). While policies can disrupt power relations, sometimes temporarily restructuring and redistributing power, the federal authority of NCLB remains substantial. Political perspectives "reveal that actors at all levels of the system can influence policy implementation" (Malen 2006, 86), while recognizing that some policy agents, such as government officials, have greater power than others. Smith (2004) situates educational policy processes as "political spectacles," in which political actors, who are cast dramaturgically in the role of policy leaders, utilize symbolic language and the illusions of rationality and democratic participation to benefit themselves (12).

Policy processes are political. Like other federal policies, NCLB enables dominant discourses to work by constructing hierarchies of normed references and making less available any kind of alternative (Shore and Wright 1997). Concepts, such as "standards-based learning" and "educated citizenry," "symbolize the increasing colonization of education policy by economic policy" (Ball 1998, 4) and set some sort of normative rationale for the actions of the state. Schools and other institutions, like supplemental educational service (SES) providers, are obliged to follow federally generated policy, as well as local (state, region, district, and school) policy. They function as the agencies through which the policy is articulated and improvisationally performed.

NCLB's seemingly unobjectionable agenda—to provide the highest quality education for "all" children in fourteen thousand districts across fifty states—prompts action, in part, by its politically persuasive wording; few, if any, would suggest leaving "some" children behind. Disguised as a solution for meeting an ever-pressing problem—school failure—NCLB, like other official policies, postures as an objective solution. Beginning with its title, which originated with the Children's Defense Fund, the policy is replete with persuasive notions and mandates.[3] A Queens assistant principal pointed out that "no one in education in his right mind would consider leaving some kids behind a bright idea" (interview, September 6, 2005). What kind of school would not want to reform itself to leave no child behind? And what would be the consequences for any school administrator who suggested that some should (and ultimately would) be left behind?

Utilizing persuasive clusters of keywords, such as "nation" and "democracy" (Williams 1976; Wright 1994), NCLB is packaged and presented to the American public as a "common sense" education reform. It is time, according to the federal government and NCLB advocates, to use "common sense" and address all of the children and help those who need it most. Common sense, "a culture-driven commodity" (Weiss 2005, 79), tells the public that those children who are failing in school need to be identified and "helped." According to Jennings, president of the Center on Education Policy, a nonpartisan group, the main concepts of NCLB are readily becoming elements of American education because the premise of attending to school failure, by targeting "disadvantaged" or "at-risk" children, have been accepted (Williams 2007). Because NCLB operates at some commonsense, anonymous level, the basic concepts are not questioned. It removes the questions of categories by naturalizing them even though it is premised on the well-honed skills of disaggregating children and their test scores into race, ethnicity, class, language, and cognitive and physical abilities so that we can make much of their differential test results. Relying on preset sociocultural categorizations, NCLB sorts out "just who is being left behind according to increasingly constrained versions of knowledge measured on high-stakes test" (McDermott and Hall 2007, 12). However, the lopsided attention given to those at the lower end of the achievement gap for several decades has done little to change the circumstances—i.e., some children are always left behind.

NCLB is built upon a reform foundation that increasingly includes corporations' interests and market-based solutions premised on the assumption that America's public school system needs outside intervention (Molnar 2005). The discourse of efficiency, accountability, and performativity surrounding NCLB and "the redefinition of education to serve the labor market has become the common vocabulary of education policies across the US" (Lipman 2000, 1). "Images of a depleted, diseased, and failed public school system, one that endangers U. S. economic health and even its national security," (Smith 2004, 14) have become engrained public assumptions. It remains so unquestioned that despite President Obama's commitment to "making every child a collective responsibility" and substantially reworking NCLB (Darling-Hammond 2009, 210), Obama "consistently argues that the relevance of education lies primarily in creating a trained workforce that will enable the United States to compete in a competitive global market"; Arnie Duncan, his education secretary, firmly supports privatization and business-style accountability (Giroux 2009, 257). Legitimized by the federal government, reform via the application of business models to education issues—standards, accountability, teacher quality, and efficient use of resources—has gained widespread bipartisan support under NCLB.

Localizing and Enacting Policy

> The No Child Left Behind Act of 2001 (NCLB) represents the most extraordinary expansion of federal power over public schools in American history. However, it relies not on the small federal bureaucracy but on state educational agencies to play the crucial role in implementing the federal mandates. . . . Under NCLB, states are required to develop testing systems. Few preferred to collect and publish sensitive racial and ethnic data, to brand their schools as failures on the basis of congressional criteria, to demand levels and timing and uniformity of educational progress that are unprecedented, to force dramatic educational change, and to be prepared to implement drastic sanctions against many of their schools and districts. (Sunderman and Orfield 2006, 526)

NCLB establishes an unprecedented national requirement for schools to meet annual achievement objectives in order to receive federal aid. The policy's standardized and high-stakes tests act as mechanisms by which the state and local educational agencies can centralize accountability and organize achievement (Valenzuela 1999; Pennington 2004; McNeil 2005; Menken 2008). NCLB and other educational policies "attempt to reduce [or, according to actor-network theory, multiply translate] the goals and purposes of education to the level of all things measurable—in this case, test scores" (Loder 2006, 31). In New York City, schools are required to administer, score, and report more than 50 million standardized tests annually to remain in compliance with NCLB assessment orders. During the last year of this study, it spent an estimated $130 million on testing (Medina 2008).[4] According to Behrent (2009), a public high school teacher, "The era of high-stakes testing in New York City has led to the creation of a plethora of predictive assessments geared at measuring students' progress toward the goals laid out by NCLB," a situation, she argues, only begets more testing (241).

Testing

Each state sets annual performance goals for schools—and for up to forty demographic groups with each school's student population, including English language learners and different racial/ethnic factions. NCLB describes performance in terms of annual measurable objectives (AMOs), which indicate the minimum percentage of students who must meet the proficiency targets. Meeting these AMOs, which increase annually until 2014 across all demographic groups, constitutes adequate yearly progress

(AYP).[5] AYP requirements are the central mechanism for improving school performances (Kim and Sunderman 2005). In fact, "schools that meet AYP requirements are assumed to be functioning well and enhancing student academic achievement. Schools that fail to make AYP are presumed to be falling short of expectations" (Linn 2008, 28).

"AYPs have been replacing the ABC's as the most important letters in many schools" (Karp 2004, 53) and, as one of the most problematic features of NCLB, they have signified school failure in both low- and high-performing schools (Au 2009). For large schools with diverse student bodies—i.e., multiple demographic groups—making AYP is far more difficult than for small schools with more homogenous student bodies (Kim and Sunderman 2005; Linn 2008). Schools serving students with achievement farthest below the AMO assigned to a given year are disadvantaged compared to those schools with student populations that are already achieving at high levels (Linn 2008).

Further, limits of AYP measures beyond the school level have also been noted. For instance, since the definition and measures of proficient achievement are set by individual states, they vary widely even though they compare current achievement to a fixed annual target. Thus, while some states have seen an increase in scores on their state assessments under NCLB, these gains have not been paralleled on National Assessment of Educational Progress (NAEP), where the achievement gap between racial groups continues to be more pronounced. Comparing trends on state assessments and NAEP before and after NCLB implementation, Lee (2008) suggests that discrepancies between the trends may lead to different assessments of NCLB's success and further confound the adequacy and utility of each assessment in measuring achievement gains.

By 2014, schools are expected to demonstrate 100 percent proficiency rates in state mathematics and reading tests in each separate demographic category of students. Schools that miss any single target for two consecutive years get placed on the schools in need of improvement (SINI) or the "failing schools" list and are required to use federal money to honor students' requests for transfers to nonfailing schools. Needing improvement for three continuous years requires schools to use federal money to provide SES. In the fourth and fifth consecutive years of failure, schools are placed in "corrective action," and by the sixth year, failing schools are deemed in need of "reconstitution," including the replacement of key, if not all, school staff.[6] "Restructuring" with an alternative form of governance begins in year 7 of a school's inability to meet its AYP goals. In this phase, the state may take control of the school and impose private management.

As noted by Sunderman and Orfield (2006), states are ultimately responsible for setting their own standards under NCLB, in addition to their state accountability goals. AYP requirements thus vary from state to state, and schools that meet high state accountability goals, but do not meet all their AYP targets, will fall into the same "failing" category as those who did not meet any targets. Many schools, according to a study by Novak and Fuller (2003), are often designated as "failing" not because tests show faltering achievement levels overall, but rather because a single student group had fallen short of a target. Group accountability targets put racially diverse schools and urban school districts at greater risk of failing AYP goals (Kim and Sunderman 2005).

Teaching

According to NCLB, all teachers were expected to be "highly qualified" by June 30, 2006. No state met the deadline. Meeting the standards of teacher quality has "become an exercise in bureaucratic compliance," according to Rotherham, a member of the Virginia Board of Education and former Clinton education adviser (Chandler 2007). On the fifth anniversary of NCLB, thirty-three states reported that at least 90 percent of their classes were taught by highly qualified teachers; by January 2007, 78 percent of New York City classes met the mandate, showing a nearly 10 percent increase from the previous year, but still nearly 8 percent less than the rest of the state. State Education Commissioner Mills stated that despite the significant progress, New York State would not be in a position to meet the one-year deadline extension and would risk losing federal funding (Andreatta 2007).

To attend to the NCLB's teacher provisions, some states lowered their certification standards or changed the process by which individuals are considered as "highly qualified." In California, for example, forty thousand teachers who had been teaching on "emergency permits" were organized into preservice or internship programs because NCLB prevents states from designating emergency-permit teachers as "highly qualified." Under NCLB, once these teachers were enrolled in preparation programs, they immediately qualified for the label of "highly qualified" despite assumingly having the same skills and experiences they did while teaching in the capacity of "emergency teachers." Texas now identifies teachers as "highly qualified" if they earn an undergraduate college degree in a field "closely related" to the subjects they teach and also if they pass one multiple-choice examination that focuses on subject-matter knowledge.

Contrastingly, NCLB's requirement that teachers demonstrate subject-matter competence on a test in each subject matter has rendered many highly accomplished teachers "unqualified." According to Margaret Spellings, the secretary of education under the administration of President George W. Bush and a proponent of NCLB, "The whole notion that you have to have grounding in the subject area that you're teaching makes a lot of sense to policymakers and to moms and dads. . . . You know, the old you-can't-teach-what-you-don't-know philosophy" (Chandler 2007). According to Spellings and NCLB, to become highly qualified, a teacher must have a college degree, a full state license, and "some" mastery of content proven either by coursework or by standardized test.

Funding

Estimates of NCLB's direct fiscal costs vary dramatically; indirect costs have, for the most part, been incalculable. In 2002, Congress authorized $18 billion for the initial authorization of NCLB, but in the first year of NCLB, the Bush administration made $624 million in cuts to the national education department's budget. The 2004 Bush administration's budget called for only $12 billion in funding. Between 2002 and 2004, the budget for NCLB was reduced as the costs of implementing NCLB increased for states. Overall, the federal government's spending on NCLB represents approximately a 1 percent increase in total school spending, leading some states, including New Hampshire, to label NCLB the "unfunded mandate" (Karp 2004, 64). In twenty-nine states, the funding for Title I grants to high-poverty schools was actually slightly reduced with NCLB. On average, funding would need to have been increased by nearly 30 percent per state in order to cover the costs of NCLB; that's nearly $130 billion additional federal dollars per year or greater than ten times the current funding level (Mathis 2003, 2004).

The SES provisions legitimize the need for resources beyond those regularly available through the school system by federally authorizing companies outside of public education to teach children directly through curricula and programs developed independently but paid for by Title I funds. The funds used for SES are reallocated from the Title I funds, which were already granted to schools but were slightly increased under NCLB;

they do not represent separate additional funds for school districts or individual schools (Sunderman 2007b). In fact, administration costs, such as parent outreach, cannot be paid from the Title I set-asides, and it is estimated that NCLB cost states nearly ten times as much as they receive from the federal government. According to NCLB, school districts must reserve 20 percent of their Title I funds to cover the cost of providing SES and the expense of transferring students out of "failing" schools, the "two high profile interventions in the early improvement stages" (Mintrop and Sunderman 2009, 355). Most districts have difficulty providing better schools to which students can transfer and across the nation, about 1 percent of eligible students choose the transfer option. In New York City, transferring to a more "successful" school, an option known as "public school choice," is not encouraged by the practices of the Department of Education (DOE); instead, the majority of funds are used to pay SES providers approximately $2,000 per child for 100 percent attendance in a tutoring program.

Enacting and Further Localizing Intersecting Policies

Multiple educational policies—federal, state, and district policies—and the practices they prompt, circulate, interact, and overlap at any one time. Often, as one shifts or changes, another fills particular practice needs, while leaving others unattended. As the meaning of one policy changes politically, its purposes are reworked and a second or third policy may be reoriented to adjust to the change. The enactment of one may support the mandates of another or contradict them. In the case of SES, school districts were responsible for implementing the regulations in ways that did not conflict with extant policies. As noted by Heinrich, Meyer, and Whitten (2009) in their mixed methods study of Milwaukee Public Schools' SES, "although after-school tutoring was not a novel intervention itself, the context in which SES programs were developed and administered under NCLB was new for state and local educational agencies and their contracted providers" (35). Further, Olsen and Sexton (2009) found policy actors within schools responding variably to NCLB directives, with individuals and particular groups, such as teachers, often quarreling over power, resources, and support.

As NCLB regulations were put into practice across the country, the New York City public school system, the nation's largest school district, was undergoing multiple changes. After being granted control of the school system, Mayor Michael Bloomberg, supported by Schools Chancellor Joel Klein, began Children First: A New Agenda for Public Education in New York City (known as Children First), a set of NCLB-aligned, standards-based organizational actions, in 2003. Developed to cure what Bloomberg stated were the school district's persistent and multiple operational, structural, and academic failures, the actions prescribed by the reforms were numerous and far-reaching. According to Bloomberg (2007), "Most importantly, everything we do, every reform we undertake, every initiative we pursue is a means to an end, and that end is giving every one of our students, regardless of personal circumstances, a fair chance at a successful, fulfilling, productive life in a world that increasingly demands unprecedented levels of knowledge and competence" (1). Along with NCLB mandates, Children First directed action at failing students in failing schools—and furthered Mayor Bloomberg's centralization (or, in Latour's words, "localization") of governance over the country's largest school district.

Much of the groundwork for Children First was laid well before its inception in 2003. Mayor Bloomberg had already been granted control of the New York City school system by the state legislature and changed the status of the "Board," which he referred to as "a rinky-dink candy store" (Traub 2005) to one of the city's departments.[7] From there, the mayor chartered an overhaul of the system—from the selection and purchase of textbooks and notepaper in the district's 1,400 schools to the reorganization of its bureaucratic structure. In an interview, one Bronx middle school principal called the reforms "an absolute takeover by the powerful business elites who run the city." Mayor Bloomberg and Chancellor Klein referred to their actions as "unifying and stabilizing."

Bloomberg's actions launched him into the national spotlight, "cementing his place at the forefront of urban education reform in America" (New York Times 2007). His reorganization and localization of the city's school system was applauded by many other cities and resonated with the national standards-based reform (SBR), which had already come to dominate in U.S. education policy. Children First reform objectives included the major principle of SBR: "State regulation of public schools should emphasize local accountability for the results of schooling, rather than inputs such as money or other resources" (McDermott 2007, 81). According to SBR, schools were able to earn rewards if students did well or be sanctioned if students' performance fell below targets. Smith and O'Day

(1991) claim that these accountability measures were intended to create a "coherent *systemic* strategy" that could combine educational reforms with state structure within a broader systemic reordering of American public schooling.

The initial Children First reforms were standards based. They directed and organized action throughout the school district. The prescribed activities and actions centered on three core principles—leadership, empowerment, and accountability. In 2003, as part of the initial reforms, Mayor Bloomberg attempted to condense the thirty-two community districts into ten bureaucratic regions, each consisting of three to four community school districts. A lawsuit blocked Bloomberg from eliminating the thirty-two districts, so the regional and district offices existed alongside each other. The superintendents resided in the ten regional offices and nearly all the bureaucratic operations were situated in the regional offices. However, during the second phase of the reforms in 2007, the centralization of power initiated in the first phase was essentially reversed. Abolishing the recently established ten regions, Bloomberg reinstated the thirty-two community districts and superintendents, added school support organizations, and integrated services.

Beginning with the second period of reforms, principals were offered three "school support organization models" designed to help schools reach their accountability targets, provide professional development and support, ensure high-quality teaching, and design programs to increase student's test scores.[8] The three models included an Empowerment Support Organization (ESO), four Learning Support Organizations (LSOs) designed by leading DOE regional superintendents, and nine Partnership Support Organizations, each an external nonprofit institute with "strong records of successfully supporting schools."[9]

Among the three models, joining the ESO—i.e., becoming an Empowerment School loosely connected to other schools—cost a school $29,500 annually; the second model ranges from $33,750 to $66,675. The Community Learning Support Organization, one of the LSOs, offered three price levels—basic, premium, and elite. Failing schools were required to purchase the elite model for $66,675, thus seemingly penalizing the schools that apparently require the greatest assistance. When asked about the greatest cost for the most failing schools, a spokesperson for the LSO explained that it takes more to help the "needy failing students" than it does other students.

Among the greatest challenges to schools and principals was implementing the standardized curriculum under Children First reforms. The "new balanced literacy" programs—a combination of fundamentals and reading and writing—was adopted in 2003 at the direction of Chancellor Klein. Offered as the single approach in all schools, the program includes writing and lengthy "literacy blocks" that focus on reading. To complement a perceived weakness in the program's fundamentals, Klein intended to add a phonics component provided by Month by Month Phonics. However, seven prominent reading researchers informed Klein that not only was the phonics program "woefully inadequate," but that it also did not meet the NCLB's requirement of using a "research-based pedagogy" (Traub 2003). To avoid losing nearly $70 million federally earmarked for reading instruction based only on "scientifically-based" curriculum, Chancellor Klein added a scientifically supported phonics program.

Overall, Children First greatly expanded the authority of principals in three areas: It awarded principals with the power to select a leadership support system, to spend funds redirected to schools, and to exert greater control over teacher recruitment, retention, and removal. With the increased autonomy came greater accountability; New York City became a school district delocalized with strong federal standardization. According to a *New York Times* article (Herszenhorn 2007), "This is supposed to be a glorious moment for principals. Mr. Bloomberg, seeking extraordinary gains in student achievement, has said principals must be elevated to a pre-eminent position in the school system's hierarchy. Yet, in interviews with principals across the city, many say they have never felt so underappreciated while their jobs have never been tougher." Several principals expressed that they were officially being held accountable for what was surely to be the national failure of NCLB. Labeling NCLB the "nation's current pastime," the dean of a Queens middle school said that principals were being made the "Fed's scapegoats" with the help of the mayor.

Principals were expected to make the changes required under NCLB and the Children First reforms—and were held to comprehensive accountability for using the reforms to increase academic achievement. Evaluations of principals' and schools' actions were reported in two ways. The annual school reports include disaggregated information on enrollment, attendance, teacher qualifications, expenditures, state and city test results across student subgroups, and achievement trends over three years. By November 2007, the New York City DOE began issuing each public school an A–F scale progress grade, based on its score in three categories: school environment (15 percent), student performance (25 percent), and student progress (60 percent).[10] While the school performance category represented students' annual standardized test scores, the category of student progress measured schools' year-to-year gains in moving students to proficient levels in ELA and math. School environment ratings were based on the results of surveys taken by parents, students, and teachers, as well as on student attendance rates. As illustrated in chapter 3, coinciding with the progress reports, principals began simultaneously discouraging enrollment in SES and encouraging students' participation in enrichment programs aimed at increasing school report card scores in the "environment" category.

Simultaneously, in addition to the NCLB and Children First mandated accountability plans, the New York Board of Regents, the state-level education governing body, also held schools accountable for performance. Those found as most failing were placed on a list of Schools under Registration Review (SURR). The six-step review process identified the worst performing schools, made the identification public, audited the schools, required the schools to develop "corrective action plans," and monitored the schools' progress. If a school failed to get 90 percent of its students meeting or exceeding state performance benchmarks after three years, the State DOE, the executive arm of the Board of Regents, revoked the school's registration and closed it permanently.[11] A school that did make adequate improvement was removed from the SURR list, but could still be under NCLB-accountability sanctions as the AYP requirements for most schools were higher than those set for SURR.

The ongoing multiplicity of educational reforms in New York serve as a reminder to the continual flow of actions, the movement of actors, the temporary associations, and the localization in policy appropriation. These new mandates deploy multiple actions from many additional entities and change much of what was already being done by actors in this study. Their practical activities were observable and recordable—i.e., traceable. Utilizing actor-network theory, this study examines the everyday enactment and appropriation of NCLB's SES provisions at a distance from prevailing educational policy studies that focus on implementation and evaluation of efficiency and outcomes. Actor-network theory (Latour 1995, 2005) provides a way to examine how policy, while made to do many things, simultaneously "makes" many actors do many things in many situations across many settings.

Enlisting Actor-Network Theory

As NCLB sets into motion and guides the negotiated actions of many, actor-network theory instructs one to follow NCLB as whole new sets of linkages between individuals, groups, and objects are generated and then act upon NCLB to change it. It takes as its field the linkages that are "renewed, recreated, defended, and modified . . . [and] also continually resisted, limited, altered, challenged" (Williams 1976, 112) as the policy is adapted over time. Actors go about their everyday activities, forging associations with other agents in dispersed agencies and blurring boundaries between government, schooling, and commerce (Shore 1997). Those studying the actor-network follow the interactions and the movement of actions across settings. The power of the theory lies in its insistence on following the ongoing processes "made up of uncertain, fragile, controversial, and ever-shifting ties" (Latour 2005, 28) rather than attempting to fit the actors and their activities into bounded categories or groups of analysis.

NCLB directs the action to be taken, but also orients what kinds of actors—referred to as "entities," "actors," or "actants"—are to be involved.[12] In actor-network theory, an actor is defined as what is made to act by many others and multiple actors are consistently deployed in any activity. Human actors in actor-networks are *"capable, knowledgeable agents"* (Giddens 1979, 254; emphasis in original), complete with vocabularies and metatheories about how agency works. They are full-blown reflexive and skillful metaphysicians and actants, able to provide accounts of their acts by drawing upon the same knowledge as is drawn upon in the production and performance of their action (Garfinkel 1967). The seemingly rational realm of activities and action, as well as actors' accounts of them, becomes a part of their efforts in attending to NCLB mandates. The processes of acting and explaining why they do what they do becomes the measures by which they are evaluated and made sense of by others. They also come to define their NCLB-related roles.

Actors contextualize their processes as a way to account for their actions across a wide array of situations and also to define the boundaries and rules of particular settings (Latour 1999, 2005). They actively construct the environments that impinge upon them and to which they then react. New York State creates standards that districts, like New York City, must codify into rules. In essence, they are required to translate them for local use. Principals, in turns, take the DOE rules and adapt them to their schools, creating teaching and testing to the standards and so on. Once schools give tests—because testing for students' proficiency in the standards becomes part of the rules—and they are scored, the results set in motion other chains of actions that redefine the boundaries and rules. Organizing themselves to attend to failure creates a sensible environment, to "work themselves and their roles out" over time. Simultaneously, actors construct social reality through their actions. Networked actors do work to maintain the network, which is then perceived as, but is not necessarily, durable.

The progressive constitution of the network relies upon negotiations in which actors assume roles according to fluctuating strategies of interaction. There is no stable presumption of the actor. The radical indeterminacy of the actor is a necessary element of the network. In this perspective, the representation of an actor is a process of delegation. What becomes significant is not dependent on actors as personalized positions, but as members of a network to which they are, even momentarily, accountable.

NCLB seeks to "influence people's indigenous norms of conduct" (Shore and Wright 1997, 6) by reorganizing what it is they often already do and reconfiguring connections they often already make, but the power of NCLB to direct action is far from complete. The policy makes certain actions more likely than others, yet the effect of putting NCLB into practice results in actions that are not always expected; "action is borrowed, distributed, suggested, influenced, dominated, betrayed, [and] translated. If an actor is said to be in an actor-network, it is first of all to underline that it represents the major source of uncertainty about the origin of action" (Latour 2005, 46). Actors, when they are able to act upon each other, are mediators who constantly reconcile and make sense of their actions, the actions of related others, and their ever changing daily situations. As mediators, they "render the movement of the social visible" (129). A network, then, is a thread of actions where each actant is treated as a full-blown mediator.

Human actor-mediators do not act alone. Objects, such as NCLB and standardized tests, with subjective investments also become actors. The nonhuman actors emerge when experiences are transcribed into artifact (the initial reports, still bearing the imprint of the author) and then into fact (a discovery now accepted by the collective as established and often no longer controversial) (Taylor and Van Every 2000). The transcription of findings, or production and validation of cultural texts, allows human

actors to interpret the setting and situation they are in according to the
policy. Object-actors help human actors make some sense of how the
federal mandates apply to them; they allow human actors to reflexively
take their everyday activities and simultaneously make "those same activities visibly-rational-and-reportable-for-all-practical purposes" (Garfinkel
1967, vii). By designating specific, rather than generic, kinds of actions
required, the trajectory of objects is traceable.

Mediating or taking action, as we have seen thus far, requires others
with whom to act and also to interpret the interaction. Yet, acting for another—an institution or a department, for example—exercises authority
that is conditional on being empowered to act for the collectivity. Acting
for another represents a collective (or macro) sense of agency in which
roles are defined by the activities the actors are in some way authorized
to perform and also by the situations in which they perform them. NCLB
acts in the name of the federal government. Likewise, when a human actor speaks with the voice of a collective, she speaks with an enhanced authority because hers is the voice of more than one person. What she says
or does has extra weight. An actor who speaks for a whole group or even
a portion of the group may evoke the name of the authority. For example,
actors who use phrases such as "the DOE considers . . ." and "NCLB
says . . ." have even more clout. The authority is already transcribed into
the collective representation. Such an actor is a "macroactor" (Callon and
Latour 1981). It is no longer just the actor who is acting, but the collective
network of people who speak through her agency, the actor-network.

Agency is located not in nonhuman objects or in human subjects, but
in the heterogeneous association of the two. Taylor and Van Every (2000)
explain:

> Agency, therefore—that which acts—is located neither in the subject nor in
> the object, but in a hybrid, a that-which-acts-for, thus literally becoming the
> agent (i.e., conforming to both of the definitions of agent offered by the dic-
> tionary: "that which acts" and "that which is empowered to act for another").
> It is the agency inscribed in the hybrid resulting from the marriage of subject
> and object that both enables human interaction to transcend itself (future
> possibility), yet also constrains it (effect of the past). It is in the materiality
> of the enabling/constraining hybrid that time and space are spanned (we
> inhabit and are enabled and constrained by a constructed environment—
> constructed by ourselves in some previous time). (161)

Agency is presented in an account as doing something. It is responsible for transforming something into something else—mediating, making a difference, and leaving traces of the changes.

Actors often mediate through "translation," which is the work of making two things that are not the same, but have corresponding properties and attributes, equivalent.[13] According to the actor-network theory, the process of translation begins with a problem, like school failure, that is deemed in need of solving. Next, there is a period of problematization, in which the primary actor (NCLB as legislated by the American government) finds relevant actors (SES providers, failing districts, failing schools, etc.) and delegates representatives from groups of actors (principals, appointed officials, tutoring managers, etc.) into roles. Actors get involved in varying degrees of investment as the primary actor uses various strategies to get them to accept their roles. Finally, actors are mobilized and begin mediating the actions of others. The process of translation is composed of multifaceted interactions in which many actors co-opt each other in the pursuit of attending to failure.

Translations often include the mobilization of nonhuman agents or objects, which have been "transcribed." For example, the experience of children not scoring well on examinations and struggling to demonstrate proficiency in English language arts and mathematics gets transcribed into school, state, and federal reports, which in turn gets transcribed into the cultural fact that children are failing and need help. It is a process through which facts are "fixed." These "fixed" facts travel from location to location and are used to create new knowledge. The transcriptions are repeatedly transferred across various situations and thus acting at a distance from the experience from which they were extracted. They are not neutral instruments. They come with properties often worked out over centuries. It is nonhuman actors that amplify and transport the actions of human actants.

According to Latour (1999, 2005), transcribed nonhuman objects tend to cross multiple specialized sites, called "oligoptica," and accumulate within particular locations, called "centers of calculation," where a state's SINI list is actually calculated, for instance. Schools and certain DOEs, where standardized tests are graded and students become categorized by levels are also centers of calculations. They are linked, through the movement of more-focused and specialized object-actors, such as school reports and SES contracts across oligoptica, including SES boardrooms and principals' offices.[14] Oligoptica only direct action as long as they remain connected through the ceaseless transport of information and action.

NCLB—like transcribed test-score reports and SES provider brochures—travel via various conduits from site to site, through oligoptica to centers of calculation, connecting the locations and leaving traces of action from one to the other. Following the movements of these actants, along with those of human actors who mobilize them, provides a view of the continuity and discontinuity among modes of actions. It also supports an examination of the way in which actors engage in temporary associations with other actors, sites, and situations.

In actor-network theory, the linkages between the local (micro) actions and cultural (macro) situations are made clear. Local actions, such as children failing in a school, "*overflow* with elements which are already in the situation coming from some other time, some other *place*, and generated by some other *agency*" (Latour 2005, 166; emphasis in original). The social and cultural contexts and frames are replaced by fully visible and empirically traceable actions. The local situation is linked to the global, called the "delocalized," by the movement of actors and materials from one place to another. Localization, despite critiques to the contrary (Rabinow and Marcus 2008), allows for thick inquiry because these localized places, the nodes of the network, are not abstractly "out there" nor are they merely frames within which face-to-face interactions are embedded. Rather, each place is a gathering of complex histopolitical, social, and cultural sets of connections.

With the actor-network, Latour (1999, 2005) joins Varenne and McDermott (1998), who have long questioned the propensity for constructing and applying categories for naming actors and then using those categories to describe, contextualize, or, worse yet, predict how these actors who are acquired by particular categories shall behave according to them. Latour does not deny the existence of a social context, but argues that actions cannot be explained by context. He contends that context has too often been summoned to hold actors in place and fix their behaviors—and argues that contexts and categories "remain much too abstract as long as they have not instantiated, mobilized, realized, or incarnated into some sort of local and lived interaction" (169). Actor-network examines connections between unstable and shifting frames of references rather than holding one context still while attempting to frame local interactions. It makes the situational context explicit by analyzing how agents interact and join together. Latour posits that "what has been designated by the term 'local interaction' is the assemblage of all the other local interactions distributed elsewhere in time and space, which have been brought to bear on the scene through the relays of various nonhuman actors" (194).

It is futile in actor-network theory to keep a site a constant location (for instance, a school or an educational policy) within which to situate localized actions (for instance, appropriating policy and attending to failure). Shore and Wright (1997) explain: "The sheer complexity of the variable meanings and sites of policy suggests they cannot be studied by participant observation in one face-to-face locality. The key is to grasp the interactions (and disjunctions) between different sites or levels in policy processes" (14). In actor-network theory, "Locals are *localized* [and] places are placed" (Latour 2005, 195).

Even with an increased presence of state and federal agencies in NCLB, local conditions dominate policy implementation (Spillane, Gomez, and Mesler 2009). "Nonlocal" actors and factors—those often considered broad or global—become localized by "localizers" or "plug-ins," which make the generic specific. "Plug-ins" are merely the transcribed objects such as NCLB, official district reports, legal tutoring contracts, standardized test scores, and school memos that are moved from place to place assisting actors in building competence to act. These plug-ins allow actors to interpret the setting and situation they are in according to the policy. They help them make some sense of how the federal mandates apply to them; these localizers allow actors to reflexively take their everyday activities and simultaneously make "those same activities visibly-rational-and-reportable-for-all-practical purposes" (Garfinkel 1967, vii). By designating the specific, rather than the generic, kinds of actions required, the plug-ins become easily traceable. As sites and situations are localized and as agents and materials are sent from one local place to another place, that which was global becomes part of the network and thus becomes localized.

Following actions emphasizes what happens at the ever-fluctuating boundaries of the network. As linkages cross oligoptica—like United Education conference rooms and DOE offices—the connections in the actor-network change and, sometimes, multiply. The boundaries of the network do not necessarily coincide with the material borders of locations; instead the boundaries of a network and the relational links between its entities are defined by a connection of "topologies." Bijker and Law (1997) describe a topology as a group logically associated and linked by a commonality. United Education and school administrations, for instance, are two topologies in the network. Teachers, who work simultaneously for the DOE and United, are another. Actants are brought into the network by their deployment, or actual employment, by the topologies. The links, like the individual entities, have properties and characteristics through which actors can perform on the rest of the network and be performed by it (7).

The actions and interactions of the actors in these topologies flow in all directions. They are not isotopic; "what is acting at the same moment in any place is coming from many other places, many distant materials, and many faraway actors" (Latour 2005, 200). Interactions are not synchronic, but rather made possible by the interplay between longer and shorting-lasting actions. Interactions are also not synoptic; some participants or actors in any action are simultaneously visible at any point. Multiple shifts in agency may also occur during action and interaction, rendering them quite heterogeneous in nature.

Thus, focusing only on face-to-face interactions cannot adequately capture the appropriation of NCLB and the ways in which it affects school failure. Taylor and Van Every (2000) remind us that "the interpretive ethnomethodological model can deal with the remarkable complexity of ordinary locally situated interactive talk . . . but it fails to account for the transcendent features of contemporary social life (158). Translation can, of course, occur in face-to-face interactions as actors make sense of their own exchanges by narrativizing them. However, interactions develop knowledge as a result of multiperson interactions in the network; making failure matter becomes a system of collective action. The knowledge developed is in a collectively known or translated language—and is performed together.

One must follow the "continuous connections leading from one local interaction to the other places, times, and agencies" (Latour 2005, 173). According to actor-network theory, "you have to follow the actors themselves, that is, try to catch up with their often wild innovations in order to learn from them what the collective existence has become in their hands, which methods they have elaborated to make it fit together, which accounts could best define the new associations that they have been forced to establish . . . to collect anew the participants in what is not—*not yet*—a sort of social realm" (12). It is the work, the movement from interaction to interaction, from translation to translation, from inscription to inscription, that is to be followed. The changes, collectively made, can be traced, and read as a transcript of what has actually occurred.

Actor-network theory, as posited by Latour (2005) and utilized in this study, is the methodological approach for ethnomethodology—"the investigation of the rational properties of indexical expressions and other practical actions as contingent ongoing accomplishments of organized artful practices of everyday life" (Garfinkel 1967, 11). Latour contends that actor-network theory draws heavily from ethnomethodology, positioning actors as possessing and proposing their own theories of action to explain behaviors and interactions. Being faithful to the insight of ethnomethodology, Latour (1999) writes: "Actors know what they do and we have to learn from them not only what they do, but how and why they do it . . . far from being a theory of the social or even worse an explanation of what makes society exert pressure on actors, it always was, and this from its inception, a crude method to learn from the actors without imposing on them a priori definition of their world-building capacities" (19–20). To trace an actor-network is to "follow how agents themselves construct their world and do not at any point make any additional assumptions about how real their associations are" (Latour 1987, 205).

What happens to school failure when many actants, across many localized sites, act is "largely a by-product, an unintended consequence of action, however rational action may have been" (Ortner 1994, 395). Following the movement of action without obligating actants' behaviors to fit into any precategorized social or cultural divisions results in something that is not always pregiven, not always expected or usual. There exists uncertainty, unpredictability, and a degree of imponderability and serendipity (Taddei 2005, 99). There are many reworkings of new relationships, associations, and groups through which actions come to "mean" different things in a multitude of mediations, interpretations, and translations. In fact, the more mediators there are, the better, and the more attachments that are made and remade, the better (Latour 2005, 217).

The next chapter examines more closely SES, the federally funded tutoring provision in NCLB, as one of the least publically opposed mandates in the legislation. In it, I demonstrate how the mostly for-profit SES industry forms temporary partnerships with schools. Organizationally, the SES programs and the failing schools consist of practical procedures for accomplishing the rational accountability of school failure as a recognizable (and necessary) feature of their situations (Garfinkel 1967, 9). At a pragmatic level, both the schools and the SES providers take action to improve their positions in the partnership rather than attending to the children NCLB says cannot "be left behind."

SUPPLEMENTING FAILURE

Providing Supplemental Educational Services

In the previous chapter, I examined the constraining features of appropriating No Child Left Behind (NCLB); in this chapter, I turn my attention to the enabling features of the same policy by examining the supplemental educational service (SES) providers, the temporary associations they make with schools, the actions these linkages seem to facilitate, and their connections to school failure.[1] More generally, this chapter looks at the ways in which SES is not exactly regulated, not exactly proven, and not exactly funded to show how some actions—which appear not exactly aimed at reducing school failure—are more common than expected. I present the actions and activities of SES providers that are made possible, if not probable, by the associations, which are both reflective of and constitutive of the local appropriation of NCLB. Emphasis is given to one provider, United Education, whose actions are illustrated ethnographically throughout the remainder of the book.

SES or "free afterschool tutoring," the alternative name by which the programs are often known, are to be offered as

academic assistance to the children of low-income parents who are attending schools that, for three consecutive years, have not made adequate
yearly progress. "Afterschool programs represent a rich and diverse network of providers that state education agencies can tap as they seek to
provide parents maximum choice among providers. Afterschool programs
have a long history of providing tutoring and enrichment programs in
the schools and communities targeted by supplemental services. They
typically offer a broad range of enrichment activities and supports that
engage children in learning in ways that differ from the regular school
day, and many have [self-]documented positive contributions to students'
academic success" (Flynn 2002, 1). Flynn's description of SES, which appeared in a policy brief published by The Financial Project, attempts to
link the extra academic assistance and activities of previous times to the
current aims of NCLB-mandated afterschool tutoring. However, SES does
not, in fact, provide a "broad range of enrichment activities," but rather
narrows the afterschool programs to include only standards-based math-
ematic, English language arts, and since 2008, science lessons. Further,
it does not hint at the complexity of processes and variety of activities
involved in SES. SES goes well beyond a "broad range of enrichment activities" to include actions by the federal government, state legislators,
educational officials, SES providers, school administrators, parents, and
students.[2]

NCLB requires failing schools to partner with SES providers to improve
students' academic achievement. These schools, in need of improvement
according to NCLB, are deemed incapable of improving through their
own efforts. Enter the SES providers to provide educational support to
students at these schools, in afterschool and weekend tutoring programs.
According to Sunderman (2007b), "the SES provisions of NCLB build on
notions that the private sector can provide services better than the public
school sector" (1). The mandated associations and the ensuing actions are
situated simultaneously within an increasingly centralized governance
of schools and a competitive free market, filled with private educational
reform remedies that fuse corporate interests with government policies.
Implementing SES, under NCLB, "is almost entirely the responsibility of
third parties, both nonfederal and nongovernmental" (Heinrich 2009, 5).

The for-profit testing and tutoring industry continues to grow, moving into a variety of services formerly provided by schools and related
community-based organizations (CBOs). During the past twenty years,

for-profit companies, like United Education, have increased their activities in public schools. Tutoring by private companies in afterschool programs is a prime example of this trend.[3] Such tutoring, which enjoys widespread adoption in middle- and upper-class families, has become increasingly legitimized under NCLB; Adler (2005) says that NCLB "has proved to be a boon to the tutoring industry." Under NCLB, schools are required to offer students federally funded SES if the school does not meet the state's adequate yearly progress goals for three consecutive years. Well-established, for-profit SES providers like United Education are favored over existing services in schools (Sunderman 2007b).

Similar to other educational policies, SES mandates assume that when low-income families gain access to the services of private educational companies in a competitive market once reserved for those who could pay for services, the student achievement gap will lesson. In the open SES market, where providers are encouraged by the U.S. Department of Education (ED) to strive for market share—to compete for students—the large national firms, like United, capture the largest shares. The tutoring industry, which has doubled in size since SES was legislated, has the potential to become a $2-billion-a-year enterprise (Saulny 2005a).[4] Additionally, those companies that offer test preparation and training for teachers, in addition to tutoring, have experienced an additional boon with NCLB's emphasis on high-stakes testing.

SES providers, which are becoming increasingly visible in the educational support industry, are diverse. Their programs fall across a broad spectrum of models, including those that are Internet supported, faith based, neighborhood specific, university associated, and "ivy league" linked. In 2004, 69 percent of the providers were private, 25 percent were school districts, 2 percent represented college or university programs, and 4 percent had unknown affiliations (Sunderman 2007b, 6). In 2005, there were 1,800 registered SES providers. During the same year, the SES providers were poised to earn nearly $200 million, with the large for-profit national companies securing one-third of the profits. One year later, in 2006, the federal government reported that there were three thousand providers across the nation. Sixty-three percent were for-profit companies; 25 percent were not-for-profit organizations; 9 percent were local educational agencies or schools, 2 percent were associated with colleges or universities; 7 percent were faith-based; and 9 percent were online businesses.[5]

In New York City, providers such as Brienza, Catapult Learning, Kaplan K12 Learning, Newton Learning, Platform Learning, the Princeton Review, Supreme Evaluation, Sylvan, and TestQuest—all private, for-profit entities—hold the majority of SES contracts. Two of the largest SES providers in New York City were established in response to NCLB and offer only SES. Many of the other large companies also offer a variety of educational supports. Nearly one-third of the SES programs in New York City offer services outside of the school, in students' homes and at learning centers. Providers offering services in schools, however, hold the market advantage as most schools prefer onsite providers.

In New York City, there has been a steady increase of SES providers. As shown in table 1, in 2002–3, there were forty-seven approved SES providers in New York City. In 2005–6, there were eighty-seven approved providers, but only fifty-two were actively providing services. By 2006–7, there were 174, although only ninety-one of these were, according to the SES provider guide given to parents, offering programs in the city.

With one-fifth of the New York City schools in need of improvement (SINI) and one-fifth of its students eligible for supplemental services, there were plenty of students at which SES providers could take aim. Annually, more than two hundred thousand New York City school children were eligible to receive additional educational support under NCLB. Table 2 shows that most eligible students did not, however, enroll in SES programs.

SES providers, who use a variety of marketing strategies to secure school contracts, are competitive. Principals of most SINI were courted repeatedly by multiple representatives from dozens of providers throughout

Table 1. Approved supplemental educational service (SES) providers, New York City, 2002–2003 to 2006–2007

Year	Approved SES providers	SES providers offering services
2002–3	47	. . .
2003–4	59	. . .
2004–5	75	45
2005–6	132	87
2006–7	174	91

Sources: http://www.emsc.nysed.gov/nyc/SES/Approved Providers/SESlist.html (retrieved May 12, 2007) and SES provider guides distributed to parents with enrollment forms annually.
Note: Ellipses indicate information is unavailable.

Table 2. Number of students eligible for supplemental educational services (SES) and number of students enrolled in SES programs in New York City, 2002–2003 to 2006–2007

Year	Eligible students	Enrolled students
2002–3	243,249	30,349
2003–4	212,607	63,000
2004–5	215,797	87,366
2005–6	223,387	81,347
2006–7	208,016	52,675

Sources: New York City and State Department of Education Web sites.

the study. Partnerships between schools and providers become official under NCLB only after principals sign short-term contractual agreements—engagement notices, extended-use site permits, security requests, and snack forms—with SES providers, who agree to provide between twenty-four and eighty hours of instruction. However, the signed agreements do not ensure that supplemental programs will be implemented. Several providers signed contracts with schools, accepted enrollment forms, and then failed to execute an actual SES program.[6] Throughout the study, SES providers and schools broke contracts without sanction—making the associations not only temporary, but also in some circumstances, tenuous. This tendency undergirds many of the actions discussed in this chapter as actors set about stabilizing the uncertainties that they have cocreated. During this study, United Education consistently partnered with twenty or more schools annually.

Being Not Exactly Regulated

NCLB gives state and district education agencies the authority for establishing and enforcing rules by which SES programs are governed. NCLB says that states are ultimately responsible for ensuring that each provider has a "demonstrated record of effectiveness in increasing student academic achievement" (Section 1116[e][12][B][i]) and "uses strategies that are high quality, based upon research, and designed to increase student academic achievement" (Section 1116[e][12][C]). However, Section 1116(e)(4)(B) notes that a state-approved provider should not be refused a permit to work in a school because the local educational agency does not agree with the design or reported effectiveness of a program. This leads some, including Patty Sullivan, the director of the Center on Education Policy, a Washington-based research group, to argue that SES is not well or consistently regulated by the federal, state, or local authorities. Sunderman (2007b) concurs, noting that "for providers, the basic requirements are minimal" (4). Providers are exempt from meeting the highly qualified instructor requirement of NCLB, are exempt from offering services for students with disabilities and "limited English proficiency," and are excused from using standardized curriculum.

Regulations and sanctions of NCLB focus on accountability, standardization, highly qualified teachers, and scientifically determined curriculum in schools, but paradoxically, no similar requirements are legislated or enforced in SES programs. There is little state or district oversight of the curriculum, lessons, and evaluative measures used by SES providers. Heinrich and her colleagues (2009) note that 'in fact, the legislation strongly discourages any attempt by states and school districts to regulate instructional choices" (5). There exists a similarly alarming absence of program evaluation, and providers are only removed if they fail—according to their own reports—to increase student achievement for two consecutive years. The Government Accountability Office (2006) survey pointed out that states had yet to report any definite assessments of SES and its impact on academic achievement among students participating in the programs. However, studies (Burch, Steinberg, and Donovan 2007, Muñoz, Marco A., A. P. Potter, and Steven M. Ross 2009, Ross et al. 2009) have pointed to difficulty for states in evaluating SES provider effectiveness and determining the impact of 40 or so hours of tutoring on academic achievement given the other confounding factors in achievement assessment.

An official with New York State's Education Department (NYSED) explained the state's position: "The state doesn't see its job as one of regulating private industries. We are here to oversee the contracts between our state's schools and these businesses" (interview, October 19, 2005). A member of the federal ED confirmed that the states, not the federal government, were responsible for working with industry leaders to implement SES, and he cautioned that too much federal regulation would be vigorously fought by the tutoring and testing industry, which would ultimately "bring SES to its knees" (interview, March 28, 2006). More succinctly stated, in the words of a Manhattan assistant principal, "They [the SES providers] don't have to do anything by the book because they don't have a book!" Indeed, while the procedural requirements, such as submitting attendance and enrolling students, are micromanaged by the DOE, the actual content of SES programs is largely unexamined.

In 2007, the heads of New York City's most prominent SES providers met in a series of meetings with the schools chancellor to create "a book." Referred to informally by SES providers as "the Klein Commission," the group met four times to draft a set of regulations and standards for providers. After three meetings, when far fewer providers, including United, were interested in the group's continuance, they drafted a letter of recommended actions and sent them to Chancellor Klein. A few of the actions were implemented in autumn 2007, but overall, the SES processes in New York City remained unchanged, prompting the United director to respond to DOE procedural restrictions with the phrase, "[That's] reason 273 why working with the DOE is hard." He became increasingly convinced that the DOE and other SES providers did not want stronger guidelines. He explained:

> The other providers were interested in getting Klein's ear, but they didn't really want change. . . . Why would they? They're slimy businessmen. You know, some of them have been found in violation of ethical practices and I hate being lumped together with them. They don't measure up. They won't. No one's going to make them. . . . If they were accountable, they'd go bankrupt and then just get a new name, new logo, and start up again. We've seen it already with [provider's name]. . . . The DOE doesn't want tougher rules even though they know we need them because they don't have any idea how to enforce them. (interview, April 24, 2007)

Even when the Education Industry Association drafted a code of ethics and behaviors by which tutoring companies would abide, New York City chose not to adopt the code for its providers.

As required by NCLB, New York City's DOE developed a monitoring system of SES. The city's DOE hired monitors, former teachers, principals, and superintendents to conduct "unannounced visits to schools to review the implementation of the SES programs that are located in the school buildings, including district programs" (e-mail from Betty Arce, the DOE director of NCLB/SES implementation until summer 2006, to all registered SES providers, dated January 23, 2006). According to the plan, monitors would visit approximately twenty schools, where they would ask to see documents such as student plans, progress reports, and attendance sheets for each SES provider. They would interview school staff and SES instructors, as well as parents and students—and observe tutoring sessions.

The observations did not yield "a book" of program guidelines consistent with research findings. New York, like other states, did not have the capacity to effectively monitor providers or conduct evaluations of the SES programs (Sunderman and Orfield 2006). Observations were sporadic, if not arbitrary. From February 2006, the month after the observations began, to June 2007, observations were made at less than ten schools where United held SES programs. These observations varied greatly in length and thoroughness. One observer asked only to see United's liability insurance, while another looked at all the United documents onsite, visited classrooms, and interviewed United supervisors and instructors.

Legally, SES providers' accountability, albeit minimal, was to state and local educational agencies and not to the individual schools or the students and their parents. Companies were approved to provide SES by New York City's DOE, and all payment transactions were centrally managed by the DOE, although SES were ultimately deducted out of each individual schools' funds. Site permits, security applications, and even snack requests, were made to the DOE, once principals had given written approval. A staff memeber of the DOE's SES department emphasized the role of the DOE during a provider meeting: "Being an SES Provider, as many of you know, is not fun. . . . It's a rule-bound program and we have lots of rules. Rules make things run more easily and allow us [DOE] to keep track of your work. . . . We need compliance. We need people [providers] who will cooperate with us. Just give us info according to the rules, when we ask. . . . It's not up to principals and schools. It's up to us" (field notes August 19, 2008). Bureaucratically, the DOE exerted authority over SES providers' actions and enforced standardized processes of permitting and record submission.

In practice, however, the DOE often deferred to individual principals when differences in expectations arose between providers and schools. Despite the oversight role of the DOE, principals, with their authority over their schools, were able to directly impact the afterschool onsite SES providers. Some principals requested modest SES program modifications; others set multiple and exacting requirements for the providers. Principals were able to dismiss providers if their expectations were unmet. The partnership between the providers and the schools was, thus, always unequal, occasionally short-lived, repeatedly discordant, and frequently wrought with misconduct.

Although there is no official procedure for reporting the daily actions of SES providers or for notifying the DOE of provider "misconduct," evidence gathered during investigations of SES programs resulted in cancellation of contracts for a few providers.[7] An investigation of certain SES providers in New York City by Richard Condon, the special commissioner of investigation for New York City School district (2006a), revealed numerous violations by providers, who "engaged in a number of questionable business practices in their dealing with the DOE, with parents of DOE students and with students themselves" (2). The practices in question included misappropriation and misuse of confidential student information, the failure to conduct background and fingerprint checks on tutors-teachers, improper parent and student solicitation, offers of money to school employees for the enrollment of students, monetary donations to schools, and the offering of self-serving incentive programs—including CD players, sporting event tickets, and $100 gift cards—tied to student attendance.

The investigation of SES provider practices began in September 2004, when one of the city's local instructional superintendents alleged that a representative of one SES provider had offered several principals $5,000 each if they enrolled 150 or more students in the program. In two interviews with investigators, with his attorney present, the representative confirmed that he had obtained students' personal information to enable his company to solicit the parents at home and that he had discussed the concept of "giving funds to schools" with principals. However, he denied that he had discussed any actual dollar amounts with any principals.

It was later revealed that the representative had provided funds to two principals. He finally admitted that he gave $2,000 to one Queens principal who he stated had solicited a "contribution to the school's renovation fund" (Condon 2006a, 5). In a second interview with investigators, the principal, under oath, admitted that he solicited funds and received a check in the amount of $2,000. He maintained that he had received permission to obtain these funds from his supervisor and then he invoked his Fifth Amendment privilege against self-incrimination, at which point he was granted immunity for his testimony against the SES provider (Condon 2006a, 14). According to the parent coordinator and assistant principal at the Queens school, the $2,000 company check was not cashed by the school; they maintained that the principal did not ask for the funds (interviews, April 2, 2007).

Another representative from the same SES provider also requested student lists containing students' addresses and telephone numbers and offered gifts of televisions to a Bronx school in order to boost student enrollment in SES. An administrator denied that such practices were company policy, but admitted to investigators that during the 2003–4 year, in violation of SES regulations, the company had offered fifteen dollars to schools parent coordinators for each student enrolled. The practice was halted after the DOE notified the company that parent coordinators, often the ones responsible for organizing enrollment in all SES programs, could not be hired by the vendor. The admission is ironic given that the chief executive of the same company was cited in a *New York Times* article as embracing a standardization of SES and code of ethics (Saulny 2005b). In the article, the executive was quoted as saying: "What's missing in our industry is this: a yardstick. . . . If this industry is going to evolve and be accepted, we're going to have to build some standards. We have to be able to say, 'Here's what success is.'"

During the same investigation, several representatives of another provider were also found to engage in questionable activities. A representative offered funds both to school administrators for increasing enrollments and also to students for attendance; "several school employees and students reported that the company offered [$100 and $50] gift certificates" (Condon 2006a, 11). The provider also persuaded parent coordinators to introduce the company to parents as "the provider of choice." In a few instances, parent coordinators placed the company's promotional information on their schools' letterheads and had the principals sign the documents before distributing them to parents. A Bronx principal admitted to doing so, and a parent coordinator in Brooklyn was instructed by her principal to give confidential student information to providers, including the provider in question.

During the 2006–7 year, a prominent SES provider employed similar practices, suggesting to schools that they be called "the premier provider."[8] At an open house meeting held at a Queen's middle school, the principal introduced the representative as "the leader of the schools premier and primary provider." The parent coordinator of this school, who was offered money for enrolling students by another company in 2004, stated that she did not receive similar offers from this representative. However, in a breach of SES regulations, the representative did receive a DOE parking permit, a desk in the parent coordinator's office, and a locked storage closet—all privileges denied to the other two SES providers at the school. In addition, the principal sold ice cream bars to the provider to raise money for the school; the ice cream was then given only to those students who enrolled in the provider's program (personal communication with principal, October 25, 2006).

The company representatives engaged in similar behaviors in other schools in 2006. At a Jackson Heights intermediate school, they hosted a parent breakfast in which the company representative gave a presentation, distributed promotional materials, and made SES enrollment forms available to parents. According to the parent coordinator and an assistant principal, the school's principal had approved the breakfast, stating that it did not violate any SES regulations. In the internal e-mail message circulated at the company, which was given to me by the school's parent coordinator, the company's representatives were told that they could indeed sponsor such events, as long as other providers had the opportunity to do likewise. The message warned, however, that the representatives should set up the events before notifying other providers; it stated, "any provider can do this. . . . We just need to get in there and do it first." Representatives from other SES providers were invited to the breakfast the day before it was held and were allowed to give presentations after the sponsoring provider had been acknowledged for its generosity and its representative had made a twenty-minute presentation. During the breakfast, the SES company that hosted the event enrolled fifty-two students; the other two onsite providers enrolled a total of six students.

Of equal seriousness, the contract with another SES provider was suspended in 2006 because the company's online tutors, whose backgrounds and fingerprints were not adequately checked, were located in India, not in Texas as stated in the contract (Herszenhorn 2006c). According to an e-mail sent to SES providers and schools by Kathleen Lawrence, the director of NCLB/SES in New York City (October 26, 2006), the provider ignored the contractually required checks and "permitted its employees located in India to directly communicate with New York City public schoolchildren through the Internet."

During the 2005–6 year, the company had been paid $2.4 million to provide online tutoring to 2,172 children in forty-four schools, but had violated state rules banning incentives by offering each student a "free" laptop computer. Essentially, an undeclared incentive that violated state rules, the laptops were delivered to students only if they completed their

SES program, thus ensuring that the company would qualify for the maximum federal funds. Further, in an investigative report to Chancellor Klein, the special commissioner of investigation for the New York City School District (Condon 2006a) stated that the company also provided schools and school administrative staff with computers that were on "permanent loan" once the school had chosen them as one of their onsite SES providers. In 2007, the company reemerged under a different name and received a contract with the city.

As shown in these examples, the actions of DOE personnel—usually principals, assistant principals, and parent coordinators—mediated or were mediated by the actions of the SES providers. According to Condon's (2006a, 2006b) investigations of SES providers, improper actions of DOE employees fell into the following broad categories. They included providing student rosters, labels with student information, and student telephone numbers; sending out flyers endorsing one provider; limiting provider selection or enrollment forms; allowing solicitation of parents and students; and accepting money from an SES provider for the school (12–13).

Being Not Exactly Funded

Nationally, the federal funds available, but not necessarily used, for SES increased 45 percent from $1.75 billion 2001 to $2.55 billion in 2005; the growth of funding was variable, with the greatest increases in the West and Southwest regions (Sunderman 2007b). Some districts actually experienced a decline in funding. In 2004–5 the U.S. ED allotted New York City more than $851 million for Title I. Eighty million dollars of it was paid to SES providers, but in the following year, slightly more than $798 million was granted (Sunderman 2007a). The amount of federal dollars paid for each student enrolled in SES also varied across the country. NCLB set the per-pupil cost for SES as the lesser of a local educational agency's per-pupil allocation under Title I, which vary from $900 to $2,400.[9] During the 2004–5 school year, SES providers in New York City were able to charge a maximum of $2,181.65 per student for 100 percent attendance. A year later, they could charge a maximum of $1,997 per child for 100 percent attendance.[10] Providers determined how much they charge to provide services to a student per hour. Thus, the number of hours of service an SES provider offered was directly related to the cost of the provider.

While federal funds allocated for SES increased, demand for SES leveled off or declined over the same time period (Sunderman 2007b), suggesting that, indeed, factors other than gross-level funding must be examined. Some have speculated that because the tutoring is not mandatory, students' participation relies on how cooperative schools are in partnering with SES providers and more heavily on whether or not the districts find the allotment of funds adequate to cover the costs of providing services to all eligible students and thus promote SES well.

NCLB stipulates that "if sufficient funds are not available to serve all eligible children . . . priority will be given to the lowest-achieving eligible students" (Section 1116 [b][10][C]).[11] School districts must set aside 20 percent of their Title I allocation to pay for public school choice and SES and are required to use at least 5 percent of these set aside funds for SES unless demand for services is low. Districts that are required to provide SES programs are instructed to use their Title I funds to cover the costs of implementing the program, which can be substantial, but they are not allowed to use the funds to pay for administrative costs, like parent outreach. In 2004–5, the Chicago School District shifted more than $2 million to administer their SES programs (Sunderman 2007b).

The monies used for SES were reallocated from the Title I funds already granted to the school and did not represent additional funding for school districts or individual schools. Peterson (2005) explains that school districts, like Chicago's, have a "clear financial disincentive" to enroll students in SES and often redirect the SES set aside to their own purposes (44). Nonetheless, districts that choose to divert SES funds are in direct violation of the law. Nearly three-fourths of the forty-five principals interviewed in this study stated that shifting Title I funds to SES actually reduced their ability to provide needed services during daytime classes and afterschool to their students. According to a Brooklyn principal,

> I could use this money to buy more students a couple of reading coaches or math experts. . . . Face it, schools don't want to give this money to multimillion dollar companies to do some elevated homework help. We know where we need the money and we aren't too happy that the feds are telling us we need to give it to SES providers. . . . So, I'm basically stuck. I've got to provide SES and I have to use some of my money. That means we won't have some programs we need in the day. (interview, August 5, 2006)

Other principals stated similar objections and petitioned the DOE for additional funding to replace the Title I funds spent on SES.

Four principals, who partnered with United, took explicit actions to minimize their SES spending, although restricting student's enrollment in SES conflicted with NCLB regulations that required districts and schools to promote maximum student participation. One, the principal of a Bronx middle school, demanded that United offer services only on Saturday despite the company's data showing dramatically lowered participation rates for Saturday programs. He told the United manager, "If I have to have you guys here, I'll have you here on the weekend. And you'll have to pay for the permit and security. You know I don't like you, don't like the whole SES thing. You cost us money and I don't think you're worth it. . . . I don't want to see you here during the week. I don't want you marketing during the week and I don't expect you to have a large program" (field notes October 22, 2008). Even though United's SES program had served more than one hundred students in 2006–7, the principal ensured a limited enrollment in the 2007–8 SES program by distributing enrollment packets only to students with low test scores.

United discussed the challenges of the Saturday program, particularly its potential to negatively impact student enrollment and attendance and asked the principal to actively support the program, through recruitment efforts and reinforcement. However, only thirty-eight students enrolled in United's Saturday SES program, which experienced a 54 percent attendance rate for the first two months of the program. In contrast, more 150 students attended the school-sponsored Saturday Academy, which had been developed and supported by the principal.

The other three principals capped SES enrollment between fifty and seventy, thus reducing the Title I funds used for SES. These actions resulted in unanticipated responses at one school—first from students' families and the school's parent-teacher association (PTA) and then from a member of the teachers' union, the United Federation of Teachers (UFT). When the principal instructed the parent coordinator to stop accepting SES enrollment forms, several parents notified the PTA president, who then instructed parents to directly contact United Education. Simultaneously, teachers who were not hired by United due to the limited student enrollment contacted their UFT representative.

The United employees who answered the parent hotline redirected the parents to the school's parent coordinator, who appealed directly to the principal to remove the limits on enrollments. The UFT representative and the PTA president also implored the principal to allow the United SES program to expand. Within weeks of the requests, the principal acquiesced and allowed forty additional students to enroll. Due, however, to their delayed start, these forty students received less than two-thirds of the program instruction, ultimately limiting some of the school's spending on SES.

By autumn 2007, the administrators, vice presidents, and president of United had begun to talk about the financial challenges faced by principals, who were required by law to reallocate their Title I funds to administering SES programs. In November, United administrators created an integrated marketing plan, in which all products and services would be marketed together, not as a package, but as possible multipronged solutions. The managers, however, continued to define their programs comparatively to other programs and often highlighted the differences in selling products and services to schools to be used during regular school hours and selling products and services for afterschool to school partners.

Principals introduced to the integrated services in the winter of 2007 were seemingly interested in having multiple United services and products in their schools, but many remained skeptical about the efficacy of the company's SES program. The assistant principal at a Bronx middle school summarized most of the concerns. She asked:

> Why should we pay for it [SES] when it isn't even proven? Basically, our school and our teachers are being told that we are incapable of turning our kids around and that we should just turn it over to SES providers when we have no idea if they are capable or not. Doesn't that sound a bit crazy to you? And then, we will just wait, holding our breaths to see if it works or not. If it does, then great. If it doesn't, we lose our jobs. . . . Who would do such a thing? We have to because the law [NCLB] tells us to. Hire multi-million dollar companies to bring in all their books and staff and just have our teachers stand by and wish for the best. Crazy. (interview, October 17, 2008)

By spring 2007, principals were undermining the SES mandates by attending to a DOE-policy-based incentive. To increase their annual progress scores, they began directing more resources toward improving school environments and targeting support to students who were on the edge of measured English language arts (ELA) and math proficiency. The New York City DOE began issuing each public school an A–F scale progress grade, based on its score in three categories: school environment (15 percent), student performance (25 percent), and student progress (60 percent). While the school performance category represented students' annual standardized test scores, the category of student progress measured schools' year-to-year gains in moving students to proficient levels in ELA and math. School environment ratings were based on the results of surveys taken by parents, students, and teachers, as well as student attendance rates.

Coinciding with the progress reports, principals began simultaneously discouraging enrollment in SES and enrolling students' participation in enrichment programs. A United manager suspected the principals were attempting to increase the "school environment" scores on the school's annual report cards. Her suspicion was confirmed by a Queens elementary teacher, who explained: "Well, it's like this. It'll be really hard for us to make too much progress in student performance. We already are doing really well this year in ELA and Math. Our kids even scored well, so we need to get points for school environment and what parents and teachers said was that there was too much test prep and not enough enrichment. So, now we have enrichment. What can I say? It's all about the scores which are tied to accountability which are tied to our budget" (interview, March 1, 2007). A Bronx principal confirmed the tactic, noting that he was also trying to raise his score by offering more diverse afterschool options. He admitted that he would "reroute" some of the federal Title I funds he was allotted for SES to administer his new programs. According to the Education Industry Association, a lobbying group for eight hundred corporate and individual SES providers, the principals in this study were not alone. The Association accused schools and districts across the country of trying to "dissuade parents from accepting tutoring on grounds that it would eat up federal aid that schools need for other reasons."[12] Similarly, the Government Accountability Office (2006) reported that school districts found SES to be a weak competitor against extracurricular and other afterschool programs.

As the DOE took actions to make schools more financially and academically accountable with the second phase of the Children First reforms in 2007, increasing numbers of principals took actions to customize the SES programs to fit within their plans. As principals struggled to incorporate (or not incorporate) SES into their plan to reach their financial and academic accountability goals, they tailored the afterschool programs to resemble the school day in overall structure, curricula, staff, and instruction. Responding to the principals increasing management of SES, a United Education vice president argued that principals had "manipulated SES into the last class of the school day."[13]

United, along with other SES providers, shared the responsibility of "extending the school day" by publishing curricular materials similar to schools, hiring teachers from the schools, and structuring their programs to reflect the organization of the school day. Consistent with NCLB rules, SES providers created or bought afterschool curricula that were aligned with the state's standards for each grade level (Section 1116[e][12][B][i]). Because is K–12 educational publishing is controlled by less than a handful of companies, many texts used in SES programs resembled, if not replicated, materials already being used during the school day and in summer school. With each set of curricula aimed at attending to state's standards, SES lesson material was similar, if not identical, in content to lessons taught during regular school hours.

The likeness of SES and daytime materials did not go unnoticed by school staff, parents, or students—but the responses to the similarities varied drastically. A parent coordinator from a Queens' elementary school well summarized the range of reactions: "Providers are smart to make their curriculum just like the schools. Principals are really looking for that. They don't want to risk something new, you know, not in these times. And it makes it easy for teachers to use if it's just like the stuff they teach all day. . . . Kids, they don't like it. I hear some of them tell their parents that SES is a waste of time because it's just like regular school" (interview, March 14, 2006). Several principals concurred that they wanted an SES curriculum as similar as possible to the daytime curriculum because they needed the reinforcement of materials. One explicitly stated that she saw SES curriculum as an extension of daytime lessons and, therefore, wanted as much consistency between the two as possible. She argued that "having SES wouldn't make sense otherwise. . . . It is to support not supplant our lessons. . . . I don't need kids getting too many new ways of doing things. . . . I don't need teachers trying to teach differently" (field notes December 2, 2006).

By the time of this study, most of the for-profit SES providers, like United, hired DOE teachers to provide SES instruction. Up until 2005, even the largest providers, including United, had hired both DOE teachers and noncertified, provider-trained instructors, but pressure by the UFT and school administrator to hire DOE teachers resulted in an SES teaching staff compromised primarily of DOE teachers. United Education held SES trainings for all interested DOE teachers at their schools, but the hiring of teachers rested less on their participation in training and timely submission of human resources documents than on the approval of principals. According to a United manager, "We train lots of teachers. Some are really great. You know, engaged and bright and alert, but most are just tired and lazy and just there for the money. . . . They know they're going to work because they're close with the principal and they [principals] have the final say. It's sad because the best teachers aren't being hired" (interview, November 8, 2005). Principals stated that they chose certain teachers because they knew them well and trusted them—and later added, because they were "good" teachers. One assistant principal, in charge of SES teacher selection, admitted, however, that he felt pressured by the principal to choose two "really bad" teachers because they were friends of the principal. It was difficult to verify that principals were basing their teacher approvals on anything other than qualifications, but United managers and teacher trainers came to call the vetting process "the buddy system."

In addition to using similar curricula and hiring DOE teachers, most SES programs also came to reflect the organization of the school day. School administrators, especially after the second implementation of Children First reforms, negotiated the structure of the SES programs with the providers. One-half of United's partner schools studied stipulated that the SES program would need to parallel the school's academic scope and sequence. Many principals were concerned about the achievement of English language learners, and most requested United to spend more time on ELA lessons until the January state ELA test even though United's SES program was designed with an equal number of ELA and math lessons.

Some principals, who had CBOs providing services during the school day, afterschool, and on the weekend, required SES providers to accommodate the CBO programs' schedules. Typically, the SES program was made to either "push services into" the CBO program or to take students out of the CBO program for an allotted amount of time. For instance, at a Brooklyn elementary school, the principal required students enrolled in United's SES to attend an hour CBO-based enrichment program directly after school, then go to SES, and finally to return to the CBO program for an hour. To accommodate the principal's arrangement with the CBO, United shortened its program hours per session from two to one and added three staff members to pick up the students from the CBO program. Shortening the daily sessions by half extended the overall program two months, and the DOE teachers, who were hired by United, protested both the program extension and the later session start time, but the principal stuck to her plan and the teachers went unpaid for the hour in between school dismissal and SES, when the children were attending the CBO program. At another Bronx school, the United SES teachers would actually enter the CBO program's rooms and teach lessons for ninety minutes. This, according to the Bronx principal, saved time and money.

And SES is only one of the options to be paid for with Title I funds under NCLB. Switching to a school that is not failing, known as "public school choice," is also possible—although this is more difficult and is not encouraged by the practices of the DOE. In a double-sided 2003 New York parent information sheet, titled "Just the Facts for NY Parents: Supplemental Educational Services," published by the NYSED, one paragraph is devoted to describing the public school choice option while the remainder of the sheet is directed towards SES. The sheet instructs parents to "learn more about supplemental educational services" by contacting their school to find out what SES are available, by going online to see the list of approved SES providers, by making a choice of SES provider, by being involved with learning about SES learning goals, and by finding out how to help their children make progress. Nowhere on the sheet are parents instructed about what to do if they want their children to transfer schools. According to the directives in the New York City DOE's "NCLB Public School Choice Parent Information" (printed in nine languages), choosing to transfer one's child to another school demands attention.

In 2005, in New York City, five thousand students requested transfers out of SINI. "All were offered the option to transfer," but by February 2005, only 551 students had been transferred and 1,965 students had enrolled in SES instead of transferring (New York City DOE 2005). In 2006–7, 6 percent or 10,832 of 185,016 eligible students applied for a transfer. Of the 6,451 offered a transfer, 2,982 accepted the offer. Among the reasons given by parents who initially chose the transfer option but did not in fact transfer their children to other schools were children's refusal, lack of school choice, distance of newly assigned school, and inevitable loss of SES. A few told me they had never received the transfer application form in the mail or had missed the deadline set less than one month from the mailing date.

A staff member of the NCLB/SES Implementation Program in New York City insisted that "public school choice is always an option and we don't discourage it—but changing a child to another school times thousands is not an easy task and it takes money from SES since they [public choice and SES] draw from the same twenty percent [of Title I funds]" (personal communication, February 8, 2006). The difficulty of transferring under the voluntary public school choice provision of NCLB was recognized by the New York City DOE, and in August 2007, Chancellor Klein announced plans to use a $2.4 million federal grant to help students transfer from low-performing to high-performing schools. Part of the plan includes offering financial incentives—namely, an additional $2,000 for every student transferred—to encourage high-performing schools, which have been reluctant to accept students, to make more places available to them. It remains to be seen if the plan will be implemented and if it will in fact increase the number of transfers. A regional superintendent pointed out the difficulty for most principals in accepting transfer students: "A principal of a successful school isn't readily eager to accept failing students who may jeopardize their [sic] school's own [adequate yearly progress evaluations]" (interview, November 15, 2005).

Being Not Exactly Proven

"When NCLB was enacted, there was no research documenting how effective SES might be for improving student achievement" (Sunderman 2007b, 5). Because SES includes tutoring and small group instruction outside of the regular school day by non-school agencies, instructional practices vary significantly (Burch 2009) and studying its impact on academic achievement has been limited and challenging. However, the number of studies aimed at investigating the effects of SES, mostly in single urban districts, has recently grown. For example, Ryan and Fatani (2005) found that students in Chicago receiving at least 40 hours of tutoring experienced greater gains in reading and mathematics than those students who did not receive SES. In their study of SES in the Los Angeles Unified School District, Rickles and Barnhart (2007) concluded that even among students with high SES attendance, the gains in academic achievement were "fairly small" and for those with lower attendance, the effects were not statistically significant. Ross et al. (2009) , in their investigation of SES in Tennessee, found that "student achievement analyses mostly showed small, nonsignificant effects of tutoring services offered b individual providers" (37). Similarly, using a mixed-method approach to evaluate the effects of SES on student achievement in Jefferson County, Kentucky, Muñoz and Ross (2009) found "no achievement advantages for the SES participants on state-mandated test scores in reading and mathematics" (22). In each of these studies, the findings are qualified by several factors, including the inability to employ randomized experimental designs.

In their study of SES in Milwaukee Public Schools, Heinrich, Meyer, and Whitten (2009) reported findings consistent with other related studies of SES in urban districts of similar size. Their empirical evidence suggested that free lunch eligible students were less likely than other students to attend SES after enrolling and students with greater absences, as well as those that have been retained were less likely to participate in SES. Among their findings, they concluded that students with greater academic need for supplemental services may not be receiving the additional tutoring NCLB intended to provide (36). However, the researchers found no "statistically significant *average* impacts" of SES on reading and math test score gains (37).

In the 2007 National Longitudinal Study of NCLB, a study commissioned by the U.S. ED, Zimmerman, Gill, Razquin, Booker, and Lockwood (2007) reported that on average, across the seven districts studied, participation in SES had a statistically significant, positive effect on students' achievement in reading and math. Comparing student achievement gains for students enrolled in SES with district mean scores, the study found that students who participated in SES for multiple years experienced the largest gains in test scores.[14]

In lieu of state-level evaluations of SES programs, most states depend on information submitted by the SES providers to monitor the efficacy of their services.[15] Unsubstantiated by independent review and studies, the data offered by the providers is used both for meeting the minimum provider guidelines issued by the U.S. ED and for marketing their programs to parents and principals. With limited monitoring by the state and local educational agencies, the accountability requirements for SES are essentially ignored. All providers claim that their services improve student achievement and make general references to the ways in which they increase students' knowledge of New York performance standards.

Some SES providers, like United, highlight the outcomes of the "independently developed tests" given to students at the beginning and the end of their SES program. United measures its efficacy by the difference between the scored pre- and posttest and selectively utilizes the improved scores in single-paged glossy marketing flyers. A flyer used during the 2007–8 school year lauded average gains of twelve points, from 48 percent on the pretests to 60 percent on the posttests. Fourth graders were cited as making the greatest increases, while third graders showed the most significant improvement in mathematics test scores. To further emphasize the test scores, a bar graph of the scores accompanies the text; however, no other "data" or information about the "research case study"—including dates, numbers of students tested, and the nature of tests—is provided.

Relying on the test scores as proof of the program's efficacy also belies the data-collection process. Despite United's attempt to uniformly proctor the examinations, students were given widely varying directives, assistance, and time limits. Throughout this study, I witnessed teachers providing students with correct answers, students sharing answers, and students being given additional time to finish questions. In contrast, I also saw numerous United instructors de-emphasize the tests, informing students that the tests weren't important and administering the examinations randomly. Many students, especially those who entered the program after its inception, were not pretested, and many students did not complete the program and were not posttested. United's director was aware that the company's SES program was unable to administer tests uniformly and commented that that was an "ongoing struggle for the entire industry."

The challenges of administering the exams notwithstanding, all SES providers are required to report the test scores to parents, to schools, and to the DOE as part of their reporting requirements. United includes the test scores, as well as attendance, on each student's progress reports and disaggregates the scores, by topic, on the school-specific annual reports. Schools, in turn, are required to place the information on their end-of-the-year reports, which the DOE then translates into various district-specific summary reports. The test scores, as part of a larger evaluation of student achievement, make it into a variety of national reports.

United's reports of improved test scores paled in comparison to the more erroneous claims made during the study by other less-established SES providers. At schools' open houses and parent-teacher meetings, representatives from multiple providers boasted about students' increased achievements. One representative from an in-home, one-on-one tutoring program told parents that students enrolled in their program "doubled their scores on state examinations." The marketing director of a large school-based SES program told principals that students who participated in his company's program "jumped, on the average, two whole levels." The first claim was impossible, and the second assertion could not be substantiated. Both representatives later reported to me that they had exaggerated, "just like the others." One said that it "just came to me on the spot, so I said it—and it might have worked. I think it got them listening."

Enacting their roles as "good," if not "the best," DOE partners under

NCLB, the SES employees organize their everyday work actions by manipulating the facts when there is no external constraint imposing exactness (not exactly regulated). They created and offered narratives for parents and school staff precisely to eliminate the actual uncertainty (not exactly proven) of their actions—and also to provide, for themselves, a strategy to manage the ambiguity in their actions. In settings, like school open houses and parent nights that are not easily recognizable as for-profit domains, there is a tendency to make less of the complexities of both school failure and the specific associations between SES providers and schools.

Schools have long been recognized as agencies through which educational policies targeted at school failure are articulated; private tutoring and testing companies have not. NCLB mandates—in particular, those associated with SES—are bringing many more actors attending to failure to the fore. As seen in this chapter, SES providers are simultaneously "passing" as legitimate educational institutions, manipulating the educational system, and attending to failure through everyday actions and activities loosely directed by NCLB.

ACCENTUATING FAILURE

Emphasizing the Need for "Help"

Attending to school failure as prescribed by No Child Left Behind (NCLB) requires timely (and timed), if not, immediate action. The issues of failure must be quickly addressed by many—
including, but of course not limited to, all those associated with
schools of education, educational support services, states' education departments, school districts, local governments, and
the testing and tutoring industry. Organizing actions along the
accountability timelines set by NCLB demands that principals
and school staff of failing schools do something without delay. If
their actions and activities do not directly increase the ability of
their school to meet their adequate yearly progress (AYP) goals
within a few years, sanctions will be imposed. For schools that
have not met their AYP goals for several consecutive years, the
stakes are even higher. Jobs can be lost and the schools restruc-
tured, closed, or put under district or private management.

While concerns about addressing school failure were ubiquitous throughout the New York City's public schools, the

administrative staffs—principals, assistant principals, parent coordinators, and deans—of certain schools expressed great alarm and called for
more immediate action. In schools where failure was made to matter
excessively, through exaggerated actions and discourses of despair, the
activities of supplemental educational services (SES) were translated as
necessary "lifelines." Of the forty-five principals and thirty-six assistant
principals I had interviewed, only six reported their school's failure to be
more notable than others. When asked to tell me about their school's academic achievement, two middle school principals said that their schools
were "failing badly"; two elementary school principals ranked their school
failure as "critical"; and one assistant principal saw his school's failure as
"important and dire." The response that seemed most fraught, however,
was given to me by the principal at Middle School (MS) 532 in Queens.
On repeated occasions, she told me, her staff, and parents: "You know
our school has very serious critical failure. We must take extraordinary
measures." Along with other members of the school's leadership team and
teaching staff, the principal interpreted the characteristics of her school's
SINI (schools in need of improvement) status into a bleak condition.

The principal's emphasis on the grim nature of failure at MS 532 and
the imperative need to attend to it resonated with the consistent warn-
ings of a national educational crisis by the testing and tutoring industry.
For nearly three decades, the federal government and the tutoring industry had pushed for more testing and increased supplemental curriculum. With the passage of NCLB, the educational support industry gained
a captive, albeit sometimes reluctant, partner—America's failing public
schools. NCLB secured the place of the industry in schooling and further
legitimized the services and products of outside, predominantly for-profit
companies.

The urgency and the problems that resulted when schools and tutoring
companies partner to fix school failure as quickly as possible are illustrated by the following three examples. The first focuses on interactions
between MS 532's principal, assistant principal, and parent coordinator,
each of whom expected United Education to be the school's "lifeline," and
the education manager, who was given the ominous task of "saving the
school" in sixty program hours. By most educational standards, MS 532
was a school in which most students were doing well. By NCLB measures,
it was failing only because one accountability subgroup had not met its
score objectives, and by 2005, the school had put into place several supports for students in this demographic. Nonetheless, the school's leader-

ship consistently emphasized the school's "extreme" need for academic assistance.

The second case follows a United manager across contexts, from MS 532 to the meeting rooms of United Education. It spotlights how the urgency prompted by NCLB and Children First reforms to "fix" schools gets translated into United's urgency to get a larger share of the tutoring market in New York City. As the SES managers discussed the best ways to improve United's position in the SES marketplace, it became clear that the company's focus on following and appropriating NCLB rules was more about ensuring the success of their operations than about "saving" children from school failure. Like other NCLB stakeholders, United had a unique purpose in implementing SES provisions.

In the final instance, I examine the ways in which the ratification of the United Federation of Teachers (UFT) contract in 2007, which was translated, transcribed, and circulated in various memos at MS 532 and United Education, among other schools and organizations, created an alteration to schooling hours that required pressing action by parents, school staff, allied staff (including bus drivers, security guards, and food service employees), and afterschool SES providers. The alteration—essentially an addition of 37.5 minutes of small group instruction to most school days for low-achieving students—was publically support by the city's Department of Education (DOE) and the state's Department of Education (NYSED) despite the disruption it caused. These examples show many people and places become connected while taking urgent, albeit disparate, actions to remedy school failure. Proceeding with speed, according to the NCLB timeline for ending school failure, creates consequential problems that, in fact, take attention away from students.

Demanding a Lifeline

When failure is exaggerated, it can lead to what the principal of MS 532 calls "a lifeline" to "needed" supplemental services. I was initially introduced to the principal by the school's parent coordinator, whom I had met at a regional SES meeting for parent coordinators and other school-based SES contacts. Within ten minutes of meeting the principal, she told me, "Just think, if we weren't a failing school now, we wouldn't be getting any of the things that we are entitled to get, the things our kids really need. Personally, I think all kids should get them, but they're going to save us for sure. . . . SES is what we need, and well, deserve. No Child says basically that it's our last hope" (interview, July 13, 2005). Throughout the 2005–6 school year, the principal would repeat similar sentiments to me. In an odd twist, she situated failure as a prerequisite for (future) success. Caught up in the crisis of failure, claiming that NCLB with its mandated tutoring and accountability would "save" her school, this principal and many of her staff "hitched a ride on the Accountability Express" (Kohn 2004, 91). Appropriating, or "taking for themselves," the SES mandates of NCLB, the school's administration team elevated the tutoring directives to a miracle-like status.

With high-stakes hopes that afterschool tutoring would help the school meet its AYP goals, MS 532 partnered with three SES companies to provide tutoring at the school. Nearly equal numbers of students enrolled in each of the three programs. Approximately 150 of the school's sixth, seventh, and eighth graders registered for the United program, and fourteen of the school's teachers were hired to teach the United curriculum. Two United supervisors managed the logistics, materials, and instructors of the program, which met on Tuesdays and Thursdays for two hours after school.

In a series of communications—e-mails, phone conversations, and face-to-face meetings—between the United manager and the school's principal, assistant principal, and parent coordinator, the "urgent need" to attend to the school's failure was at the fore. The magnitude of perceived need was explicit during the initial SES program planning meeting in August 2005. As the principal and the manager of United's SES program met to discuss the program logistics, the conversation began with a discussion of the school's need for help:

> *Principal (P):* We really need you here! We have had very serious critical failures and now we need to do something about them. We've done all we can, believe me. It isn't like I have a staff that sits around waiting for things to get better. I have real go-getters, but when you do as much as you can and still fail it's time to get help. . . . I'm choosing United because of your record in the region and because, well, I've heard that you accommodate what we want.
>
> *Manager (M):* We're glad to partner with 532. . . . We'll be able to help your students.
>
> *P:* Good. We want it all. All the best that you have. You know, books, testing skills, and any other tricks of the trade for high scores that you can teach. I'm counting on you to save this school.

M: We'll do our best. We have a remarkably user-friendly curriculum. . . . It's standards-based and has helped other schools in your situation . . .

P: Right, so I just want to say again how much we are expecting you to do wonders here with our lowest [scoring] students. Our own academy, run by [the assistant principal], will take care of the fours [highest scoring students] and the other provider will help the threes. . . . You will teach only those students who need the most help. So you see why I'm putting my faith in you. I have to.

The belief that MS 532 could be "saved" by United was consistently reiterated by the school's principal. It was, according to the United manager, "relentless, a real overstatement of need and expectation by the principal, who kept spreading the message of crisis."

Interactions between the United Education manager and MS 532 staff members demonstrate that it was not only the principal who was translating low test scores and unmet AYP goals into critical need for intervention. The actions of the school's parent coordinator, in particular, seemed to reflect the urgency. The following e-mail exchange during November 1–9, 2005, between the parent coordinator and the United manager illustrates this:

Parent Coordinator (PC): I do not understand why you are not running your program on parent meeting night. The other providers are having their programs and I don't see why you can't.

Manager (M): . . . United does not hold our program during parent meeting nights at any of our partner schools. In particular, at MS 532, your teachers who instruct our SES classes are not available because they will be meeting with parents. . . . The United SES program calendar, which was given to students, parents, and school administrators prior to the start of the program last month, clearly indicates that we will not be having program on that date. . . . We will also send voiceshots to parents, in Spanish and English, reminding them of this . . .

PC: Well, I don't care what the calendar says. I've been telling the parents that your program will run that day because we can't spare any instruction time. Don't you remember how much we need your services? It doesn't look good if you take a day off so early in the program. I don't think the principal will approve either. She's counting on you and don't think I won't tell her!

United did not hold its SES program on the parent-teacher night, but the manager and another United representative did give a brief presentation at the event.

During the event, the principal introduced the United manager as "one of the school's greatest hopes for success." Ironically, the parent coordinator refused to talk to the manager or sign up any more students for United's SES program. The following day, a parent called the United office to complain that she had been discouraged from signing up for the "most hopeful program." This was in direct violation of SES regulations, and, eventually, the principal interceded and directed the parent coordinator to "let go of her grudge." However, United Education received no more enrollment forms.

At the end of the SES program, after sixty hours of instruction had been provided and the state examinations had been taken, the principal requested another sixty hours. She asked the manager: "Is it possible to continue for another sixty hours? From March 14 until May 30?" The manager replied that United, like all other SES providers, received federal payment only for the number of hours (measured in quarter hours) each enrolled student attended, up to the total number of contracted hours—in United's contract, sixty hours. Still, the principal made additional requests, asking United to extend its program at her school. She cited low test scores and the "exceptional need" of her students to start preparing for the following year's examinations as the primary reason to continue the school's relationship with United. When repeatedly told that United could not, according to its contract with the DOE, extend any programs, the principal charged United with having a bias against the school.

Both the assistant principal and the principal accused United of "abandoning" them by ending the program after the contracted sixty hours of lessons. In an interview, the assistant principal stated, "You know, we knew that they were going to teach for sixty hours, but that doesn't help our students who need more than sixty hours of instruction. . . . You'd think they might think of the students, but I know it is about money. . . . We wanted them to stay until the end of the year to give us a fighting chance for next year. . . . This isn't just a business with us. It is about saving kids' futures. . . . We bet that United would help us. . . . We can't wait until the next year" (April 2, 2006). Others in the school, including two deans and one literacy coach, echoed the assistant principal's sentiments.

Along with the principal, they expressed their fear about taking preventative measures in the spring to increase student achievement in the following year without the assistance of an SES provider. However, the school continued its own academy, in which ten of the school's teachers extended their daytime curriculum afterschool, until the beginning of June, because they "couldn't wait until the next fall." At the parent meeting in March, near the end of the United's program, the principal began "selling" her own Saturday academy to the parents as the "program that would save the school from failure." In comparison, United Education, which was once seen as the "lifeline," was portrayed, at the same meeting, as part of the problem due to its "early" end date.

The urgent need for educational supports and assistance directed further actions even though the school had yet to receive the results of its 2005–6 state examinations and thus could not calculate its AYP goals. The school staff—predominantly, the principal, the assistant principal, and the parent coordinator—continued to cast MS 532 as a school in dire need of improvement and the students as requiring immediate academic intervention. The message and the staff's actions were consistent from previous years. They had become part and parcel of the everyday work situation at the school—actively renewing the need to fix the school's failure and reflexively constructing practical reasons for the staff's actions.

Failure at MS 532 had become fact more than a year earlier, even though, according to the 2003–04 annual report for the school, MS 532 had actually met most of its AYP goals and fell short of meeting its mathematics and English goals in only one accountability group—English language learners, who represented less than 17 percent of the school's total population. Seventy percent of this subgroup performed at or above grade level, and the subgroup demonstrated consistent increases in state test scores from 2002 to 2004. Compared to similar schools in the district, MS 532 was in no greater need of academic intervention or support. By most measures, MS 532 was better situated than many schools on the SINI list.

Potential failure at the school continued to be emphasized—made more than what it was—by the MS 532 staff. Even when the 2004–5 and 2005–6 state examinations showed improvements at the school, actions at MS 532 became more deeply embedded in a mock-up of their need. They were involved in the "serious game" (Ortner 2003) of attending to school failure in an arrangement where the practical activities of schools and SES providers were directed to attend to failure, "very seriously critical" or not. Their everyday work situations became a policy-driven "activity system" (Lave and Wenger 1991) for those deemed in need. Through their actions, the staff constructed the reality of ominous failure even as new information, such as the 2006 examination scores, showed things to be otherwise. As new information arose, it was interpreted in terms of the pattern of urgent need that had become commonplace.

The tensions, complexities, and contradictions in the appropriation of NCLB at MS 532 demonstrate how language is repeatedly used as a norming agent. The discourse at the school, which included the "urgent" rhetoric, gave the impression of universal or homogeneous failure that hid the possibility of differences that existed at the school. The message of crisis circulated throughout the school in memorandums, electronic messages, and conversations that were "plugged" into meetings, trainings, and announcements.

Positioning MS 532's failure as extraordinary triggered an unexpected response. Prior to the 2006–7 school year, under the public school choice option provided by NCLB, fifty-three MS 532 parents requested that their children be transferred out of the school to a school that was not on the SINI list. Twenty-four of the parents had enrolled their children in the Strategy SES program the previous year, and twenty-seven had enrolled their children in the other two SES programs. All except two parents gave similar reasons for the transfer request. They stated that they did not see the excessive focus on testing, tutoring, and other academic interventions implemented at the school as necessary or desirable.

The grandparent and guardian of an eighth grader at MS 532 chose to transfer her grandchild because of the school's "unbearable focus on making children feel bad about their test scores." Every week, her grand-daughter lamented that the school was pushing her too hard even though she had been designated a level 4 student and was performing well above grade level in both mathematics and English language arts (ELA). In an interview, the grandmother explained why MS 532 was no longer the right school for her granddaughter.

> *Grandparent (GP):* I used to like this school. We did. . . . And then all this
> school does now is push, push, push. I don't think my [grand]child
> deserves that kind of thing. No one really does. She scores the highest
> on all her tests, but the school wants her, well everyone to do better.
> She can't. How does the best do better? See what I mean?
> *Researcher (R):* Yes.
> *GP:* If you are doing really well, you shouldn't be told that you need to do
> so much better for the school?

R: For the school?

GP: Yeah. The principal and that dean is always saying "Do it for the school. Help set Good examples for your classmates who aren't as smart as you . . ."

R: Hmm. That must be difficult for her.

GP: It is. It really is. You know, she is a good kid and she doesn't need that kind of thing from her school. We push her hard enough at home because of her mother and all being gone. (June 3, 2006)

United was also concerned about the school's insistence on its failure, but benefitted financially from the large student enrollment in the program. The principal chose not to partner with United in the upcoming year despite the reassurance by a newly hired United manager that the company could offer a second session in the spring. In the autumn of 2007, however, MS 532's principal contacted United and invited them to an SES provider fair. United declined the invitation, but in making its decision, the tales of the partnership with MS 532 were recirculated. More senior managers, including the one who had been directly involved with the SES program at MS 532, told recently hired managers about the school's previous demand for attention.

The United managers began referring to an account of SES policy mandates in which they constructed schools, like MS 532, as "crisis-oriented, SES failure fanatics." As the particular version of "policy as discourse" (Ball 2006) circulated among less-experienced staff members, it achieved the elevated status as an SES "truth" and was often employed by them to talk about schools in general. As the novice managers met with their program supervisors, several warned that schools were likely overemphasizing their SES need in order to get more United services. One of these managers cautioned that the SES mandates gave authority to "all of the greedy, overly demanding, and crisis-oriented principals of the world." It became common "knowledge" throughout United's SES division that most principals seeking SES partnerships were unfairly empowered by the policy directives. The construction, sometimes the demonization, of *all* schools as similar to MS 532 oriented the managers' behaviors toward them.

However, discourses are often discordant and contradictory. The leadership team at MS 532, especially the parent coordinator, set into motion a discourse about the SES directives based on their partnership with United Education. It was seemingly incoherent with the one developed and spread by United managers. While at a regional parent-coordinator meeting, held in late spring 2007, the parent coordinator complained about the SES mandates being "overwhelmingly in favor of the SES providers." She argued, along with her fellow coordinators, that SES companies and, in particular, United, because of its market dominance, were advantaged by the tutoring directives and, further, that they were using the rules to their advantage. In this particular topology of parent coordinators, the discursive power—who had the authority to speak, when, where, and with whom—displaced the alternate United discourse and likely informed the policy behaviors of the coordinators as they returned to their individual schools and partnered with SES providers. Clearly, the policy was being presented (and represented) differently by different actors, all of whom were trying to comply with the federal regulations.

Securing a Market Share

Interestingly, United manufactured its own discourse of crisis—translating the need to attend to failure into the need to increase their SES accounts—that mediated its actions in its partnerships with public schools. The excerpts from United meetings reveal the ways in which the imperative need to attend to school failure was inextricably bound to the necessity of increasing the market share in afterschool tutoring.

SES Manager Meeting, October 2005

> *SES Director (D):* Well, how we doing with the three Ps—parents, parent coordinators, and principals? Are we out there getting the word out that their kids need our services as soon as possible? Are we making inroads?
>
> *Manager 1 (M1):* We've [the field staff] been in schools, pushing product, and services, getting enrollments, meeting principals, leaving flyers, you know . . .
>
> *Manager 2 (M2):* But are we making ground? I keep hearing that Absolute Education is directly mailing flyers to homes. How are they getting the labels, I mean the addresses from schools? Contact information is not to be given to providers. I don't understand how they keep getting one up on us!
>
> *D:* They cheat. We don't.

Manager 3 (M3): Absolute is a small player with some tricks. We can't waste our time trying to go head to head with them. They do their thing. We do ours. . . . Our message is and should be that we have the curriculum and teachers that can turn performance around quickly.

D: Do you think we should sell the quick-fix approach? I think it's dangerous. Do we have any data to show that we can fix things quickly?

M2: Not really, but parents and schools want to hear that we do.

M3: They want to see us out there hustling our butts off to get the account and to get enrollments and to market to parents.

M1: Look, supply and demand says that we need to be competitive. There are a hundred of us [SES providers] in the city and all parents and principals do is sit and wait for us to come calling. They've got power. We have the solutions, but they tell us when, where, how much . . .

D: So, let's focus on getting to them [principals]. Let's start asking what can we do, together, now? We can't lose the competitive edge because we are in wait mode. Be proactive.

SES Manager Meeting, October 2006

Manager 2 (M2): They're [the DOE] really pushing the AYPs this year. Yesterday two principals asked me how we were going to help them reach their AYPs. . . . I don't remember that being such an out there issue last year.

Director (D): So what'd you tell them? How does United help?

Manager 3 (M3): You know, the usual stuff about research-driven, standards-based, proven results. . . . I told them that we get quick results because we've had so much experience with getting students ready to take tests in short courses.

D: Maybe we should play up our ability to get results quickly. How long are our test prep courses usually? A few months, right? So, let's use that to our advantage. We need to keep a competitive edge.

Manager 4: We're on track to meet our market goals this year, so whatever you're doing keep it up.

D: What would be gained by the quick fix slant?

M3: Schools already expect a quick fix. NCLB demands urgent action. We only offer fifty to sixty hour solutions. . . . Remember that school, MS 532? They wanted miracles and in sixty little hours. That's quick in DOE terms.

Manager 5: We shouldn't talk about quick fixes. They don't last. It sounds like cramming or memorizing is our methodology . . .

M2: You worry too much. That's what schools want, quick fixes, immediate help. Let's be realistic here. We serve the DOE.

Manager Meeting with United Education's President, November 2007

Prompted by a competitor's announcement at their public shareholders meeting that their SES enrollments had increased 55 percent, United's SES managers were called to meet with the company's president. The managers discussed the comparatively low SES enrollments: 1404 students had enrolled in United's SES, but nearly 250 more students had been enrolled by a similar date the prior year. Multiple reasons—NCLB fatigue, no enrollment deadline, cautious principals, lack of marketing opportunities, lack of enrollment forms—were given to the president.

President (Pr): Well let's set one [an enrollment deadline].

Director (D): Okay.

Manager 1: After parent-teacher conferences in November. That's our best last chance to get more [students] enrolled.

Pr: Dates?

Manager 2: For public schools, the thirteenth and fourteenth. Middle schools, where we usually get a two-fold increase in numbers, November nineteenth and twentieth. . . . We're staffing these events now.

Manager 6 (M6): What can we do differently to hype up the urgency? There's no need to keep dragging this out. Parents need to take action here and we need to tell them to do it now.

D: Flyers can read something like "Seats limited. Enroll now while there are still places available."

Pr: Okay, if the DOE can't set a deadline, we'll manufacture one. We have to do something to build momentum. We'll lose 1.5 million in revenue at this sluggish pace . . .

M6: Are we setting a deadline and if so, how can we legitimately communicate this? All the principals know that there's no deadline for real.

Pr: We'll just make our own deadline. That's fine. But let's just leave it vague and stir up some urgency. . . . "It's getting critical for your kids to sign up. Sign up now while there's space sort of thing."

Together, the three meetings, each held one year later than the previous one, demonstrate the common discourse of urgency circulated at United, especially in the SES department and among managers, where activities transition from marketing to enrollment every October and November. Even at the highest level of management, getting enrollments and thus, revenue, was determined to be one of the company's most important goals.

Keeping and increasing market share in the tutoring industry became a common thread of discussion, illuminating the stake that United attached to the SES directives and their subsequent adaptations. Focusing on the relationship between United Education and its goal of capitalizing the SES market, as shown in the meetings, revealed that they were "guided by not only their stated goals but also their inherent desire for continued existence" (Olsen and Sexton 2009, 13). The survival of United Education's SES division became the main work for involved United actors and overrode reaching the stated policy objectives (Scott 2008). And, in the meeting rooms of United Education, with the company's narrowly focused oligopticon vision, the need to maintain and increase SES accounts with schools was explicit.

At schools, when the United supervisors and instructors met every day after the tutoring sessions, a direct link was made between helping kids and helping United's competitive edge. The following excerpts from one of these meetings at a Bronx elementary school underline the translation between the need for test preparation and the need to keep the business partnership with the school.

> *Supervisor (S):* I see some of you dogging in your lessons, dragging your feet through it like it's killing you. There is no pep in some of your lessons. This isn't time to slack. The [state] tests are in less than one month and this is our last chance to help these kids.
>
> *Instructor 1:* Have you noticed how rowdy and restless they are? Two of them crawled into the closet today and the rest of them howled and howled. How should I teach them in the closet?
>
> *Instructor 2:* They've been prepared and tested and prepared all day. We aren't getting them anything they really need.
>
> *S:* Okay, maybe, but we can't let our guard down. We are a company that provides quality services. Parents expect it and the school, they asked us back this year instead of our competitors because of our great lessons. . . . It's up to all of us to keep up with the United image. . . . We

can't afford to lose this school [as an account] (field notes, December
18, 2007).

The supervisor was likely repeating what he had heard in meetings with
his manager and conversations with the office staff. In weekly conferences, the supervisors were told how important it was to be a good partner, "to provide good service and keep the schools as partners." To ensure
continued partnerships, the program supervisors were directed to get
"good" test results from the children despite the director's voiced belief
that no matter how well students did, schools just picked providers they
liked.

The annual company meeting of 2006 showcased the associations
made by United's SES staff between the urgent need for their services
and the company's urgent need to hold on to or increase its market share.
Full-time United employees who worked in New York City listened as the
company's leaders connected the need for increased educational services
for failing students with the need to offset disappointing sales with controlled expenses and increased SES accounts. The president stated that
disappointing sales were offset by controlled expenses and the success of
SES, which surpassed expectation by netting $2 million more than the
previous year. He concluded by stating that the company "urgently needed
to capitalize on SES." He then gestured to one of the vice presidents to
take the microphone to "explain our [the company's] next moves."

> *Vice President:* The further evaluation and maturation of United as a busi-
> ness remains our top priority as we go forward. We need to rework
> some of our sales plans and target particular untapped and upcoming
> markets. . . . We'll drive greater ownership, empowerment, and ac-
> countability to make the three businesses stand alone—and we'll do it
> quickly to match the pace and needs of our main client, the DOE.

Adopting the language set forth in NCLB and Children First reforms,
the vice president stressed accountability and empowerment in getting
future market shares without time to spare. Just as the DOE used these
terms to construct its message of urgency, United, at the highest levels
of management, wove its story of necessary "action steps." Accountability—especially performance targets, pressures, and sanctions—that had
reshaped schooling (Mintrop and Sunderman 2009) would be used to
restyle United's behaviors. He continued:

Vice President: We need to do better, much better, much more quickly than we now have the capacity to do. Not harder, just more quickly and more in line with what the market demands—and the market, our biggest client, the DOE, demands quick turn around and the ability to adapt to changes right now. We focus on building the capacity to be a better vendor. We'll use the SES model throughout the company. Immediate focus will breed success in a way we have never yet experienced. . . . I'm excited. I want you to be excited. (March 2, 2006)

The success or profitability of SES, highlighted by the vice president, soon caused unintended consequences for the SES staff. Managers, who spent most of their time developing relationships with school administrators and supervising SES programs at schools, were now recruited to facilitate professional development for other departmental employees. This often pulled them away from their work and caused them to work additional hours or leave SES work undone. Because of their success, the SES department faced higher enrollment targets and partnership goals, but had its operating budget cut to offset losses in product sales.

In the summer of 2007, United's SES began selling itself to schools as the flexible provider that could customize its tutoring to meet the school's needs. Managers began talking about the curriculum—the same curriculum it had used for three years—as "customized." If principals requested changes to the standard twice-weekly, two-hour sessions, United accommodated them. If principals requested changes in the curriculum's scope and sequence, a team of SES staff members worked to change them. Customization was, at first, seemingly arbitrary, and changes were made by managers, case by case, without consultation with United's administrative leaders.

In general, to meet principals' requests or demands for personalized curriculum, the SES staff became much more reactive to the actions of the DOE, which increasingly exerted itself as a mediator. Using concepts such as "standards-based learning" and "data-driven curriculum," buzz words in the DOE and at the state's education department, United set forth a normative rationale for its practical actions. As the competition among SES providers increased, actors at United used the concepts in "strategic and tactical ways, according to their perceptions of the field, while taking into account the background of their current status, and available resources and agendas" (Taddei 2005, 96). This became their everyday work.

With the increasing constraints placed on SES programs by a newly instituted DOE SES administrator, the distribution of decision making seemed to tilt further away from SES providers toward principals. United managers, trying to accommodate the principal's requests while following the DOE regulations, frequently reworked company policies and altered company procedures. At times, the changes in practice seemed to shift the meaning and objectives of the NCLB mandates—moving SES from supplemental support to direct intervention aimed at one demographic subgroups. The policy interplay between DOE structures and the agency of key policy mediators became obvious as various SES configurations were negotiated and compromises were accepted.

Adding 37.5 Minutes of Instruction

In October 2005, the new UFT contract required teachers to work two extra days and an additional fifty minutes a week. Combined with one hundred additional minutes from the previous contract, the extra time was then divided into 37.5-minute daily session between Monday and Thursday. The additional session would "substantially increase the time teachers spend on instruction, especially for struggling students," according to the DOE.[1] The addition of 150 minutes each week for small group instruction for "students in danger of not meeting standards"—i.e., those scoring 1's and 2's on the state examinations—was implemented in February 2006.[2] Attendance at these sessions was made mandatory for students identified by principals as struggling or failing academically.

Several principals and assistant principals concurred with Randi Weingarten, the UFT president, who stated that it was important to start the additional instruction as soon as possible because the students needed it. The principal of a Manhattan elementary school echoed the importance of starting the tutorials:

> Sure, it'd be easier for us to just start next fall. We'd have more time to arrange our schedules, get rooms, and explain it all to parents and everything, but we don't have that kind of time. If we're going to get kids to pass tests and if we principals are going to be held responsible, then its time the teachers also put in some more effort. I don't mean to say they haven't. Most have, but they are overloaded in the day. The extra time will be more focused on getting these kids to pass the tests and this is something that needs to happen this year, not the next. (interview, November 17, 2005)

The additional minutes of instruction were posited as a necessary intervention, beginning in February, even though the statewide ELA examinations were given in January and the mathematics tests would be administered in March. When asked about the timing of the schedule change, an assistant principal at a Bronx middle school stated that the additional instruction would be used to "cram" for the math tests. He couldn't think of better timing, noting that after a school is on the SINI list, each test becomes more important and preparation becomes all the more critical.

Others disagreed, noting that the disruption to the daily schedule would likely hurt and not help kids as they prepared for the examinations. The parent association at a Brooklyn middle school encouraged parents not to allow their children to attend the additional 37.5-minute tutoring. They distributed flyers that read: "Now they've gone too far! Too much testing! Too much tutoring!" The association mounted a campaign, and at the beginning of the first scheduled 37.5 minutes instruction session, nearly one-third of the parents arrived at school to take their children home. These children did not attend United's SES program that day, consequently, dropping enrollment from eighty-two the previous week to fifty-nine.

In general, the change in schedules caused confusion for parents, teachers, and SES providers, as some students were required to attend the additional 37.5-minute sessions and others were not. Further, some schools used the "school-based option" to add the extra session to the morning rather than afterschool. Other schools added the time to three days of the week; some added the time to four days of the week. A few schools actually staggered the days of the week by grade level. According to a *New York Times* article, "The changes upended the routines of parents, educators, school bus companies, and after-school programs" (Herszenhorn 2006a).

Like other onsite SES providers, United Education had to change the structure of its SES sessions, staggering program times to accommodate both the students who attended the mandated school tutoring and those who did not. I first learned of the addition of the 37.5 minutes from a memorandum circulating at United Education. In it, a manager pointed to the need for longer coverage by site supervisors and instructors and modifications of class rosters, use of classrooms, snack distribution, and dismissal procedures. The UFT-contracted tutoring required an overhaul of SES activities at United.

The change was described by a manager as "a logistics nightmare that challenged the cognitive capacities of the kids." He expounded:

How can we expect kids, some of them little kids, to come to eat breakfast in the morning, go to school all day, then go to nearly forty more minutes of tutoring, and then come to us for two more hours of tutoring? Who are we kidding? Kids can't learn like this. And what are we supposed to do to the kids who aren't mandated to go to the extra DOE tutoring? We can't take them up to their rooms and start our program because their teachers will be doing the other tutoring and there will be no rooms. Are they just going to sit in the cafeteria for forty minutes, I mean thirty-seven and a half? I'm confused at how this is going to work and I'm responsible for seven programs in seven schools. (interview, December 1, 2006)

Numerous parents shared the field manager's concern for the children's ability to "take in" so much information in one afternoon. United's SES parent hotline logged 227 calls the week after the UFT plan was publicized. The average number of calls to the hotline during program operation was six. Clearly, there were concerns about the additional tutoring and the schedule change.

From a business operations perspective, the schedule changes demanded a refurbishing of United's billing and calculations of program hours. Students who were not mandated to attend the additional 37.5 minutes were to go instead to the SES program for the additional time, but this was incompatible with the DOE database in which United was required to log attendance. The database would not allow changes to be made in program times or hours. So, the additional time spent by the "nonmandated students," a label that was used throughout schools and SES programs, was not billable. Yet, United was required to provide staff and instruction for the nonmandated students. At some schools, the impact was minimal as most students were mandated. At other schools, mostly middle schools, nearly one-third of the students were not mandated. Some of them left the school, rather than attend SES for additional time. Many complained to the SES staff that since they weren't mandated by the school to have extra tutoring, they shouldn't have to have it in SES either. United was, however, bound to provide instruction from the time of dismissal and also hoped that by doing so, they would prevent students from leaving the school and not returning 37.5 minutes later for the SES program.

United's program suffered after the schedule change. Some students, mandated and nonmandated, dropped out of the SES program. Others, mostly nonmandated seventh and eighth graders, left school and didn't return for the SES program. The volume of students who were enrolled but not attending SES soared in February and March. Adhering to their policy of contacting parents when students are absent, United hired a part-time staff member solely to make these calls. After a call was left on the answering machine of an absent student's home phone, the following response was left on the parent hotline: "What do you think, you people at schools? My daughter can't go to extended day [37.5 minutes] and then go to two hours of more tutoring. Do you have any idea how long that makes her school day? I don't know about you, but when I went to school, I came home before dark. She goes to school in the dark and comes home in the dark. . . . She studies all the time and I don't want her at your program so don't call to remind me again" (March 3, 2006). A parent coordinator confirmed that some parents thought that the 37.5 minutes of instruction replaced the afterschool tutoring, so they picked their children up prior to the start of the SES sessions. Others said that their children would not be safe walking home so late after the extended day and SES, so they chose to have the students attend SES only when they could pick them up.

Beyond the initial confusion and added expenses for numerous agencies and families, the limited capacity of the extra sessions—set by the UFT contract as ten pupils per class—guaranteed that some "failing" students in the "neediest" schools did not receive tutoring. Some "successful" students in the "best" schools would receive enhanced instruction, like math clubs, using the same 37.5 minutes. Simultaneously, while Chancellor Klein was referring to the contract changes as "really a landmark and indeed a truly ground-shifting effort," a member of his staff admitted that tens of thousands of children with failing test scores would not benefit from the additional sessions. When questioned about the disparity, she explained that there were just too many students to help right now. "As our reforms work," she said, "within a couple of years, we'll have fewer students in need and will be giving extra help those who need it." She reminded me that addressing failure in the country's largest district was no simple task and that they were doing everything they could to solve the problem.

The extended day was situated as one more solution to an ongoing problem—school failure—which needed immediate actions. Deputy Mayor Dennis Walcott, Bloomberg's top educational advisor, said that the additional instruction fit well with the "bold changes" already made by the mayor. In his words, "It gets to the heart of the problem. We still have some kids who desperately need more help." According to Klein (2007), the Bloomberg and Klein administration "fundamentally rejected 'incrementalism' as a strategy—a better program here, a little tinkering there. Across this great country, we've been doing just that in education for at least 30 years. And it has failed—to our shame as a nation" (2). Several city council members also applauded the additional instruction, noting that the present is the time for radical change, including providing failing students with additional time and resources as soon as possible.

The NYSED, responsible for overseeing every level of education in New York, supported the local DOEs to legitimize the additional 37.5 instructional minutes to the general public. According to an employee of the state education department, "Our focus is less about regulating the district and more about making sure their decisions are carried out smoothly and timely. We're about schools and students and doing our part to make good changes. This [additional 37.5 minutes] is a good change that needs to happen now, without delay. . . . Each month we lose preparing rather than implementing this change, could, for all we know, result in more students failing. . . . We know it is causing some havoc, for families and bus drivers and other people, but that's temporary" (personal communication, February 3, 2006). In the name of taking urgent action, both the state and local educational officials oriented their actions around creating and conforming to the rules associated with the additional minutes, possibly at the expense of the relationships with parents and school-allied businesses.

By the time United sent out letters to parents explaining the change in their program hours, the DOE, the schools, and the SES providers had negotiated the collision of policies by interpreting their changed circumstances and adjusting their actions. They had, in meetings and correspondence, explicitly taken each other into account. The letter, however, did not include the interpretive and interactional history. The circulation and enactment of the UFT contract, which rendered the SES contract impractical, if not impossible, to execute was strategically ignored in the letter as not to "confuse" parents.

Reforms made by the DOE, as much as federal policy like NCLB, served to regulate the efficiency of a mass cultural system that operated on multilateral legislative and organizational levels. Failing schools and SES providers became obliged to adhere to NCLB, as well as to state, region, district, and school policy. In so doing, they forwarded the particular version of attending to failure—the one in which adding tutoring and small group instruction to the daytime instruction of students in failing schools was seen as a remedy. For their efforts, for changing their way of doing things, schools were often promised improved "results," and SES providers were told to anticipate financial gain and market share. The SES providers, MS 532, and the UFT came to terms with "practical circumstances as a texture of relevances" (Garfinkel 1967). Teachers were working under a new contract that created a set of problems to which many needed to turn their attentions.

The delocalization of policy actions did not make it easier to fix the problem. Rather it allowed the actors to do what "ought" to be done. They interpreted "accountability" and "empowerment" variably to do their work. Actants pragmatically adjusted to the daily situations created by the appropriation of NCLB—by the actions taken by many other actors. Their flexibility was practical and required, but nonetheless, their actions provided little, if any, relief from the problem at hand—school failure. In fact, attending to failure with (hyper)urgency led to the construction of more failure. The next chapter demonstrates how not attending to failure with urgency, actually ignoring failure, produces much of the same.

NEGLECTING FAILURE

Ignoring the Need for "Help"

Given the aims of No Child Left Behind (NCLB), one might expect that attending to school failure in all schools in need of improvment (SINI) would be made a priority throughout the New York City school district. In this chapter, however, the failure—and the legislated necessity of attending to it—are minimized, masked, or disregarded, even though, by NCLB measures, it is more substantial than the failure seen in the previous chapter. Unlike the failure illustrated in chapter 4, the failure examined in this chapter is nearly neglected. Given the same and even more obvious signs of school failure, actors in the forthcoming examples take actions different from those in the previously discussed cases. The juxtaposition of the stated goal to fix failure and the daily actions in which failure was admittedly ignored illuminates the ways in which failure was made to matter through neglectful actions and inactions. The three cases that follow demonstrate that failure can be constructed, through everyday actions, as something quite different from "critical."

In the first example, Public School (PS) 472 was prompted, both by its failing circumstance and a written order from a regional superintendent, to partner immediately with a supplemental educational services (SES) provider. The school's principal initially contacted United on a day when I was interviewing managers at the main office. Then she expressed her enthusiastic desire to have the company provide SES at PS 472. Yet, as I soon discovered, partnering with United to get educational support for its student population, half of which had tested below grade proficiency, conflicted with the school's ongoing relationship with Great Works, a community-based organization (CBO) housed in the school. Clashes quickly ignited as diverse stakeholders from the CBO and United sought to enact their interpretation of supplemental education at PS 472. Partnering with an SES provider required the administration of PS 472 to engage in a series of actions that ironically ultimately dicounted the need of attending to failure. This led to a myriad of problems for themselves, Great Works, the Department of Education (DOE), United Education— and the children, who were literally left behind when the tutoring program, which was never fully implemented, ended prematurely.

While NCLB places emphasis on ensuring a highly qualified teaching staff in schools, the DOE set minimal requirements for SES instructors. The second example of this chapter examines how United Education neglected the failing scores of prospective instructors' prescreening tests and later hired the instructors who failed the tests to teach the very material on which they had failed to exhibit proficiency. The exam questions— taken directly from an eighth-grade mathematics and English language arts (ELA) state test—were administered during the hiring process and were initially intended to eliminate candidates from employment. However, the tests were presented to the prospective instructors as a normative exercise rather than an evaluative measure. This led to an arbitrary use of the test scores in hiring decisions and ultimately teaching assignments. In their SES classes, five of the instructors, whose test failure was ignored by the United managers, either excluded teaching the material or provided incorrect explanations to their students.

The final case in this chapter shows how the very organization, the DOE, responsible for distributing SES enrollment forms in New York City, created procedures that, in fact, reduced the number of students who received services. Throughout the study, there was an overall inconsistent, if not arbitrary, allocation of forms to many of the schools in the study, including PS 427 and Middle School 532 from the previous chapter. Some schools received twice as many forms as they had students. Others received less than one-third the number they needed. Further, some schools received enrollment forms in languages other than English, although the majority of their students spoke English as a first language. Focusing on the process by which the DOE dispensed or did not dispense the SES application packets to students and their families led me to discover that some schools were just not giving out the forms. In contrast, other schools and SES providers were illegally reproducing forms, which were then identified as fraudulent by the DOE and destroyed. Both actions excluded thousands of eligible students from enrolling in SES from fall 2005 to fall 2008.

Triangulating Associations

Prior to NCLB, PS 472, a Brooklyn school located at the edge of one of the borough's housing developments, had partnered with Great Works, a CBO that provided daily afterschool and weekend activities for students and adult development classes for their parents. Great Works had also helped families of PS 472 access medical and social services. At PS 472, the staff of Great Works had developed strong ties to the students, the parents, the community, and the school administration. According to the PS 472 parent coordinator, a lifelong resident of the neighborhood: "They've [Great Works] done a lot for us. That is, except raise test scores. They're, between you and me, they don't have what it takes." Great Works had been reliable in providing particular services to the students and their families, but had not implemented a strong academic component.

Great Works limited enrollment in their student programs to two hundred and carried a waiting list of twenty to twenty-five students. The program operated an in-school center in a large first-floor room, complete with necessary office equipment supplied by the school. The center was staffed by a full-time program director, his administrative assistant, student supervisors, and occasional parent volunteers. Students participating in the Great Works program snacked and engaged in activities, including Monopoly and homework help under the supervision of high school students, hired as counselors by the CBO. Grouped into classes of twenty to twenty-five students, the Great Works program occupied most of the first-floor classrooms in the school from 3 to 6 p.m.

By the fall of 2005, Great Works had been unable to develop a state-approved SES component, so the school entered into contract with United to provide SES at the school.[1] During the initial planning meeting the principal, the assistant principal, and one of United's managers agreed that United would hold its program on Mondays and Wednesdays. Simultaneously, Great Works would continue their program Mondays through Fridays. Any student enrolled in Great Works who signed up for SES would attend United's SES Mondays and Wednesdays for two hours and remain in the Great Works program the remaining days and one hour after SES on Mondays and Wednesdays. Students who were not enrolled in Great Works would only attend United's program Mondays and Wednesdays.

Within weeks of their agreement with United, the principal and assistant principal made changes to the initial plan. They decided that students enrolled with United would remain in the Great Works classrooms on Mondays and Wednesdays. The United instructors would "push into the classes" to teach with the assistance of the Great Works counselors. The United field manager was notified of the requested change by a voice mail left by the assistant principal, who concluded that the change was necessary so that Great Works could fulfill the hours of their program.

In an online chat the day following the requested change, the assistant principal encouraged the United manager to accept the change—and to bill the DOE according to the original two-hour lesson plan even though Untied would not be providing two hours of instruction.

> *Assistant Principal (AP):* It's okay. Don't worry. The kids will go one hour to Great Works and then your teachers can go into the rooms and teach for an hour for SES.
>
> *Manager 4 (M4):* But our program runs for two hours—one ELA and one Math—and we do not want to be in the rooms with other programs. I'm sure Great Works doesn't want us in their rooms either. They do art and games and sports. We teach math and ELA. How can that work?
>
> *AP:* Well, we don't have any more rooms and so that has to happen. Don't worry. I'll talk to them [Great Works staff] and we'll work it out. You can bill for two hours. It's okay. It's taken care of.
>
> *M4:* That is not what was agreed upon during our program planning meeting. You knew our program was a sixty hour program split into two-hour sessions, not one hour and we are not authorized to have other, non-United staff in our rooms. We can only bill for time spent with the kids teaching them math and English.
>
> *AP:* Don't worry. Bill them as usual. (September 28, 2005)

The discussion ended with the manager telling the assistant principal that she was unhappy about the change in hours, was not able to bill for services rendered, and was not prepared to accept the change, which would ultimately need to be approved by the director, to whom she would later speak.

Beyond the reduction in lesson time, the administration's change was multiply problematic, according to the field manager. First, some of the students in the Great Works classrooms had not, in fact, signed up for United services so were not authorized, according to NCLB and SES regulations, to be receiving United instruction. Likewise, some students that enrolled in United's SES program were not enrolled in the Great Works program. Further, the twenty students in Great Works classrooms were twice the number optimal for United instruction, which had some individualized components. Finally, United could not employ the Great Works counselors nor could the company be held responsible for their actions in the classroom.

In conversations with the manager and the director of United's SES, the principal conceded that her plan seemed not to satisfy the program needs of United, but said there was no other choice for students in Great Works. Despite the manager's protest, United acquiesced to the change in program. To accommodate the reduction in lesson hours, United proposed extending its program into June so that it could complete and legitimately bill for its contracted hours.

The principal assigned separate areas for students who would enroll in United but were not participants in Great Works; the assigned spaces, however, were not classrooms and were found, by the United manager, supervisors, and instructors, to be inadequate, if not dangerous. The spaces included a gymnasium foyer with no windows, chairs, or tables; a closed and locked hallway where fertilizer was stored; a corner of the cafeteria; a small office with one table; and a corner of the parent coordinator's busy office. Complaints by the manager yielded the use of an additional two rooms—a computer room and large storage closet, which housed two large photocopy machines. Neither of the two new rooms had usable tables. None of the spaces had chalkboards or whiteboards.

When the United program began in October 2005, tables and chairs were moved by the United coordinators and instructors into the spaces on program days—but often they could not find enough chairs. Again, the United staff, and now the students, complained about the inadequacy of the spaces. One week after the program began, two students became ill after sitting next to the fertilizer in the hallway, and the instructor experienced severe headaches. The manager refused to have a class in that hallway and instead moved the class to a table in the cafeteria. The refusal and subsequent request for different room assignments prompted a series of discussions about the assigned spaces between the United manager, the program director of Great Works, and the assistant principal, who was assigned by the principal to act as the main SES liaison for the school.

The following excerpts from a series of e-mails, dated November 18 to December 6, 2005, highlight the space limitations and the increasing tensions between the Great Works and United.

Great Works program director to United manager and supervisors:

> Hi there all. I wanted to touch base with you folks to discuss room assignments. I wasn't quite sure which rooms or areas you folks were using with children who do not attend our program. The reason why I am asking this is because we need to have a sense of which rooms or areas are being used and are free so that I can shuffle groups as need be. Also, we are trying to make sure that School Safety has a sense of which children are receiving services from United but do not necessarily attend our program.

United manager response:

> Thank you for contacting us. I need to have another conversation with the assistant principal regarding our rooms. Currently the spaces assigned to us are not adequate for teaching. None of these rooms has seating/table space or board space. . . . I will let you know what happens after I talk to the AP on Monday.

The AP cancelled the meeting set for Monday, prompting a series of voice mail exchanges between the AP and the manager and the following e-mail from the manager to the AP and principal.

> Monday, November, 21, 2005
> We need more/better rooms and spaces to hold the United classes for the non–Great Works students. United curriculum touches multiple learning modalities—auditory, tactile, etc. . . . so we need, atleast [sic] a board/writing space for teachers and tables. They foyer is okay when it has chars [sic] and tables set up in it, but does not have a board. Also Great Works holds a dance

class next door and the music blasts higher than our teacher's voices. Room 108 is a bit small and often has other people using it and the parent coordinator room is okay, but also crowded with other groups. Some suggestions: we could run the United program for non Great Works students on Tuesdays and Thursdays or on Saturday and use classrooms not used on those days (are there any?) or we need to have classrooms on another floor. I know you are working your best with what, to date, is available, but it is a priority to United to provide consistent, safe, and stable learning environments. We don't yet have these at PS 472. So, let's talk and see what options we have.

The e-mail and follow-up afternoon meeting yielded no changes in room assignments, prompting another series of e-mail communications in which the situation was repeatedly deconstructed. The principal and assistant principal remained steadfast about keeping all afterschool activities on the first floor despite an unused second floor, filled with classrooms. in the school.

The problems that occurred with teaching the students in the Great Works program rivaled the inadequate space as concerns for United. There were two serious complaints: First, SES instruction was allotted only one hour and, second, Great Works staff members were physically restraining/disciplining students during SES time.

E-mail from PS 472 principal to United manager and Great Works program director:

Monday, December 5, 2005

Please let me know when we can all set up a meeting to discuss the partnership model we outlined originally. . . . In particular, I would like to discuss the ways the staff of both United and Great Works Services can work together with regard to student conduct and fitting United into the philosophy of our school's mission. I would like to have a sit down meeting with regard to procedures for building on the strengths of the existing program and the expectations we have of a fully realized partnership between both organizations.

Great Works counselors, according to the United supervisors, instructors, and manager, physically restrained students during United's classes and disrupted teaching by yelling profanity at students who were not paying attention to lessons. Excerpts from a letter sent from United supervisors to the director explain the difficulties.

Monday, December 5, 2005

Dear [name of director]

The situation at PS 472 has gotten progressively worse. The frustration that we have experienced over the past few weeks has reached its boiling point today. United hired us (coordinators and teachers) because the company believed that we were capable of handling our positions. We have gone way past the call of duty with this site but now we just cannot continue. It is simply not feasible. There are a great number of obstacles in our way. . . . Our main concern is for the students who are being cheated out of an academically challenging curriculum. One that has been praised by numerous parents, staff, and teachers at the school. . . . It is not a positive environment for anyone involved, especially not the kids. . . . Please see below for our specific list of grievances.

1. Insufficient rooms/space for students NOT participating in the Great Works (GW) program. . . . The cafeteria and all of the other rooms that we have had to use are not conducive to learning. They are noisy, unkempt, and disruptive and lack basic resources such as a chalkboard.

2. The United teachers who are going into the Great Works rooms have been in ongoing struggles with the GW staff. The GW staff has been defiant, disrespectful, and hostile. We are under the impression that they are purposefully inciting the students to act out when United is in the room. . . . One GW counselor took one of our students out of the classroom with his arms wrapped around his neck and gripping his hands. The student was crying and other students were screaming. . . . Another GW counselor shoved one of our students against the wall because he was talking. It took myself and another coordinator to talk him into releasing the student. . . . I am aware United staff is not allowed to physically restrain or grab uncooperative students and we do not want GW counselors treating students in our classes in this way.

3. More GW students [who are in the rooms we go into teach in] are not enrolled in United than are enrolled. Thus, we are illegally serving many students whose parents have not chosen us as a provider. The kids whose parents have not enrolled them in United are essentially held "prisoner" in that room for an hour lesson. They are expected to behave and defer to our rules even though we technically do not have the jurisdiction over them. They are not our students and it is a huge liability to teach them when their parents have specifically refused our services.

The letter made clear that not only was the Great Works–United compromise not attending to the children's academic difficulties, it was in jeopardy of ignoring the students' physical well-being.

The day after receiving the letter, December 6, 2005, the director and the manager sent a letter to the administration of PS 472 and the Great Works director, requesting their "immediate assistance" in order for United to continue its program at the school. In the letter, the unacceptable teaching locations and the behavior of the Great Works staff was addressed. The letter closed by stating that while United wanted to continue providing quality services to the students of PS 472, the company would be forced to discontinue services at the school if these conditions persisted.

On December 13, a meeting was held at the school to review what had become a significant problem for United, the school, Great Works, and the DOE, who had been notified of the trouble by PS 472's principal. During the meeting, the DOE administrator agreed with the United manager that the teaching conditions were unacceptable and suggested that United offer its program on Saturdays when Great Works would not be providing services. On December 15, one of United's vice presidents sent a letter to the principal offering the Saturday program. The letter went unanswered, the DOE released United from its contract with PS 472, and United stopped providing afterschool services prior to the program's completion.

On the last day that United held SES, the day before the winter holiday break, many of the eighty-one students enrolled in United's program and the United staff expressed anger and sadness over the program's end. Several United instructors received thank you notes from parents, and one received a homemade cake. Some children cried when they left; one third-grade girl clung tightly to the leg of her United instructor, pleading her not to go. Even as the staff was leaving the school building, the parent coordinator begged the manager to continue the program after the holiday break. She pleaded: "You know this about the principal and her craziness. She has to do whatever it takes to keep Great Works, but that doesn't mean the kids who need tutoring should end up empty. . . . You know she [the principal] won't get another SES for them. She never really wanted one and now you're leaving." The manager said she was sorry and left the building with the rest of the United staff.

All adults present on this last day of SES noted the neglect of children, whose actions had not factored into the decision to end the program.

The children, who had been deemed failing and in need of tutoring, would be denied SES because the adults, who had turned their attention toward "fixing" the failure, had made so many more problems for each other—and more important to this examination—had neglected to address the students' failure in the ways expected. The practical circumstances had transformed the condition of failure. Each entity had taken actions to carry out its work, but this had not guaranteed the formation of a three-way collective. Appropriating NCLB through PS 472 produced social relationships between Great Works, United Education, and the school that were more limited in their existence than could be anticipated by policy mandates. NCLB created "landing strips for other entities [namely, United] to enter the collective" (Latour 2005, 239). It also created strips for departures. Tracing the departures, the changes, in the actor-network became part of the appropriation of NCLB and the attention to school failure that moved through PS 472.

Throughout the tenuous association between PS 472 and United, NCLB was refracted in multiple trajectories in the form of smaller texts, which, once localized, took on a life of their own, often challenging the aims of the original policy. The policy texts or scripts were "encoded in complex ways (via struggles, compromises, authoritative public interpretations and reinterpretations) and decoded in complex ways (via actor's interpretations and meanings in relation to their history, experiences, skills, resources and context)" (Ball 2006, 44). As each text circulated and became modified through particular readings of it, the resulting transcript reflected the compromises made during the practical sense making of the actor's work. Since the actors could not necessarily control the meanings of their texts, even when they aimed to exert their authority, the policy transcriptions gained their own momentum, guiding action and molding SES behaviors, both expected and unintended.

Passing as and Being Passed Off as Skilled Teachers

Hiring, training, and retaining a skilled part-time, seasonal work force to teach United SES lessons is one of the company's, if not the industry's, largest ongoing challenges. The eligibility requirements, as listed in New York City's education law, the regulations of the commissioner of education, and chancellor's regulations C-105, for non-DOE employees who are hired to work as SES instructors, requires no particular education or experience. Rather, the requirements demand that prospective instructors pass a fingerprint and security check, which are conducted by the DOE's Division of Human Resources' Office of Personnel Investigations and are paid by the SES providers. All hired SES staff must be issued a photo identification badge by the provider, and the failure to have all staff members cleared by security prior to any student contact results in the withholding of payment or the termination of contract.

Given the NCLB stipulation of having highly qualified teachers in failing schools, it is remarkable that the legislation does not also require SES instructors to have any teaching experience. Minimally, the instructors, who at United were hired in numbers between one and three hundred during this study and received no greater than twenty-five dollars per instruction hour, needed to pass initial company interviews, twelve hours of training, and evaluations—and also to be cleared to work with children in schools through a DOE-determined background check, initiated by fingerprinting. All of that, however, did not necessarily ensure that they were qualified to teach ELA and mathematics to students in failing schools. United, like many other SES companies, also hired teachers who worked in the schools where the SES programs were provided. The DOE teachers, hired by United, exhibited variable skill levels, but all were certified as teachers and were well acquainted with NCLB, the state's standards, Children First reforms, and the city's curriculum.

Until 2005, DOE teachers across the country could be hired by SES providers as instructors regardless of the status of their district, but the schools in failing districts could not, under the law, offer services using their own teachers. New York City sought and received a waiver in November 2005, the third city to do so after Chicago and Boston. In March of the same year, the United Federation of Teachers (UFT), the city teachers' union, was approved to provide SES, under the provider name of "United Federation of Teachers 'Young People's Academy.'" After the UFT received approval, Randi Weingarten, the UFT president, was quoted in the *New York Times* as having said, "We wanted to compete with these private firms that had no connection to the schools, and we were given the green light" (Saulny 2005). Many principals in this study agreed, requesting United only hire DOE teachers on staff at their schools to instruct SES.

Still, during the 2004–5 school year, non-DOE instructors were being hired by United. Some demonstrated a lack of ELA or mathematics knowledge while teaching the SES lessons, so in September 2005, a written assessment including twenty ELA and twenty mathematics questions, written at the state's eighth-grade level of proficiency, was added to the instructor training. The examination, which was intended to eliminate—or "weed out"—candidates from employment as SES instructors, was given at the end of the initial instructor. (Mis)represented to the prospective instructors as a normative exercise, the test measured their abilities to perform materials that they might be required to teach, if hired.

The examination, which was implemented by the academics team without notifying other members of the United staff, prompted a debate during a September 15 staff meeting:

> *Director (D):* The quiz won't just be normative. We'll use it to test them, to evaluate their abilities.
>
> *Trainer 1 (TR1):* But, we didn't tell them that. It's not ethical.
>
> *D:* Well, we don't have to tell them it's evaluative. It's our test. We can use it for whatever we like.
>
> *Manager 2 (M2):* If we don't hire them, we do not need to tell them that it's because they failed the test.
>
> *TR1:* Not fair. Why would we do that?
>
> *Manager 4 (M4):* Holy shit! We are testing them and not telling them and then not hiring them. What do you want us to do with that? Sounds like lawsuit territory, huh?
>
> *Trainer 2:* Yeah. Let's just tell them. Be upfront and like say we need to test your skills if you're going to teach kids.
>
> *M2:* Well from now on we will, but up to now, we haven't.
>
> *M4:* How are we going to tell them? Who's going to tell them?
>
> *TR1:* And what are we going to tell the DOE when they ask what qualifications our instructors have? They do ask, you know.
>
> *D:* We don't want teachers who fail the quiz, so it makes sense that we screen. I'm just not sure how legal it is to use the examination across the board to make decisions.
>
> *M2:* Right, some can pass the test, but are not well-suited to work with kids. . . . We'll figure out how to deliver the information [about the examination].

Despite the concerns expressed, the examination was presented as a normative exercise—and over time, many potential instructors who failed the examination were hired based on their "outstanding" presentations.

They were told that they failed the examination, but that their failure was ignored because of their "overall presentation as a teacher."

The arbitrary use of test scores in hiring decisions resulted in a handful of United instructors who were assigned to teach the eighth-grade material on which they had not demonstrated adequate knowledge. Most who failed the examination but succeeded in providing exceptional mock minilessons during training were assigned to teach grades 3 through 5. Of those who failed the examination, slightly less than one-third were assigned to teach eighth-grade classes. I followed these teachers to their SES classrooms to examine how they would, indeed, "perform" (Goffman 1959) their roles as instructors, especially when teaching the material they did not seem to know.

In one class, the instructor, who had failed the mathematics portion of the assessment, directed students to solve the expression $10 - [24 \div (3 + 5)]$ by performing all the operations from left to right. In the same lesson, the teacher explained that the order of operations was unnecessary to learn as operations—addition, subtraction, division, and multiplication—can be performed from left to right. This is not accurate.[2] When the students used the instructor's method to solve examination questions, incorrect answers resulted. Reviewing the answers with his class, the same instructor told the students that the "machine which scanned the answer sheets must have made a mistake." He noted that it was impossible for him and all of his students to get the "same exact wrong answer." "Clearly," he said, "there is a problem in scoring, not in our math." Again, not accurate.

Similarly, an instructor, who attempted to teach converting fractions to decimals, told her students that she was giving them a "new, better way to do fractions." As she converted the fraction 18/30 to 0.3 "because 6 goes into 18 three times and it also goes evenly into 30," two students corrected her. One of the students rose to the board and said "see how to do it" as he wrote, "18/30 divided by 3/3 = 6/10 = 0.6." The teacher was unconvinced by the student's method even though several students agreed that his answer was correct. She insisted that her way worked and argued with the students for fifteen minutes until class dismissal. At the following session, only one of the nine regularly attending students showed up for class. When the teacher asked the student the whereabouts of the other students, the student replied that they weren't coming back until she learned her math. She didn't, but four of the students returned the following week at their parents' insistence.

In another eighth-grade class, an instructor who had failed the ELA portion of the prescreen examination chose either to skip the content that she didn't understand or presented it incorrectly. When asked why she had skipped two lessons of material, she stated that "those things don't really help kids pass their tests." "Those things"—persuasive essays and structure in formal writing—were in fact elements of the state's examinations.

The same teacher attempted to teach a lesson on genre, which she pronounced "jen-ree," and defined as "the generalities, the general ideas of certain kinds of writings." After introducing the lesson topic with her definition, the following dialogue ensued:

> *Student 1 (S1):* Uhm, I think genre means type, like fiction or mystery.
> *Student 2 (S2):* Yeah, it means like kind, a kind of story. I mean, I like horror stories but not romance novels.
> *Instructor (I):* Well, yeah, but it's about the generalities of those kinds of stories.
> *S2:* Huh? Not really, it's the kind of themes, right?
> *I:* Okay, so we have it. Let's move on . . . Okay write down the genres or general ideas of the story we read earlier.
> *S1:* Plot?
> *I:* Sure, if you think plot is a general idea.

The class ended with some students writing the plot, or "jenree" according to the teacher, in their workbooks and others making a list of genres, including "fiction," and "poetry."

It was apparent to me that the instructors were not able to teach certain topics, but the failure of these instructors, who were hired to directly attend to, if not fix, school failure, was repeatedly neglected. The five instructors I followed, like all other United instructors, were observed twice during the year by a United manager. All but one received passable marks and all were retained until the end of the program despite complaints by students and students' parents.[3]

The students assigned to these instructors seemed to fare less well; one-half of the forty- four students did not complete the SES program during the 2005–6 year. An experienced United instructor gave a plausible explanation for the higher than normal dropout rate in her colleague's class. She reasoned:

Well, loads of kids dropped out because frankly their teacher didn't really know enough. I tried to help him, but he was, well, weak on his math knowledge and skills. What are the kids going to do? Keep coming and unlearn all the math they know only to get taught the wrong formulas. I wanted those kids to come to my class, but I teach sixth grade. I saw that teacher struggling and I told the coordinator to move him to elementary or something. I don't even like to be associated in the same program with him. (interview, March 5, 2006)

Students were likely most affected by United's neglect of the instructors' ineptitudes. If these students were failing, there was little, if anything, to indicate that the instruction they received, or did not receive, by these instructors helped them not fail.

These United instructors were "passing" as people who were teaching "well enough." United was "passing them off" as teachers who were teaching well enough. Theirs was the work of achieving and securing their positions "while providing for the possibility of detection and ruin carried out within the socially structured conditions in which this work occurred" (Garfinkel 1967, 118). They were also passing and being passed off as actors attending to failure. To comply with the legitimate expectations of United, the partner school, and NCLB mandates, they were doing the "unavoidable work of coming to terms with practical circumstance" (Garfinkel 1967, 185). They were using the skills they had, in the ways they knew how, to do the jobs they had been hired to do.

NCLB, like all policy, has gaps of ambiguity—spaces in which actors can take "charge" and establish, for themselves and often others, elements of the policy that may or may not be in line with the initial stated aims of NCLB. Federal policies, like NCLB, conflate the specific and the general. In this case, the training of the United instructors, which was subject to specific measures and evaluations, got folded into more general NCLB processes. Sunderman (2008) notes that when aiming to attain the high standards and bring the proficiency of all students up with the tools and requirements specified by NCLB, "the devil is in the details" (1). Training and hiring qualified SES instructors was one such detail that became ignored in a broader view of policy implementation that focused more on sanction-driven outcomes than processes. However, this particular appropriation of the SES mandates points to the fissures between the formal policy, the discourses that surround it, and their diffuse practical application.

Distributing Enrollment Forms

The Education Industry Association, a lobbying group for eight hundred corporate and individual SES providers, suggests that some schools and districts in fact "dissuade parents from accepting tutoring on grounds that it would eat up federal aid that schools need for other reasons."[4] Across the country, nearly 2 million students qualify for free tutoring, but according to the DOE's more recent data, only 226,000 or nearly 12 percent, enrolled in SES programs in the school year that ended in 2004. A 2007 report, extracted from the National Longitudinal Study of NCLB and prepared for the U.S. DOE, found that 24–28 percent of eligible students in grades 2–5 participate, while fewer than 5 percent of eligible students in higher grades enroll in SES (Zimmer, Gill, Razquin, Booker, and Lockwood 2007).

Despite a 20 percent increase in SES enrollments nationwide in 2005–6, the proportion of eligible students using the services dropped 5 percent even as the total number of eligible students increased from the 2004–5 year. Recent data (Sunderman 2007b) shows that as federal funds for SES have increased and more students have become eligible nationwide, there has simultaneously been a decline or leveling off of demand for SES. National trends demonstrate that overall, there are more students receiving services, but they represent a smaller portion of those eligible. The number of students reportedly receiving services in New York City, however, decreased, even though more students were eligible.

In New York City, the number of eligible students has fluctuated between 243,249 in 2002–3 and 208,016 in 2006–7; however, the number of enrolled students dropped each year since 2003–4, when nearly eighty-seven thousand students were signed up for SES. Over four years, as the number of eligible students increased steadily in the city, those who actually enrolled, decreased. The greatest decrease of fourteen thousand students was experienced in 2006–7, prompting United's SES managers to accuse the DOE of mishandling enrollment forms—i.e., providing an insufficient number of forms and not regulating how and when schools distributed the forms.

United's SES director repeatedly railed against the DOE for not providing enough forms and held it responsible for the decrease in enrollment numbers in 2006–7. During a staff meeting, he lamented: "So, they [DOE] say they want us to enroll more students, but they aren't giving schools forms. No forms, no students. Low overall enrollment numbers this year. It's an easy equation, in that sense. Schools have asked, right? And they haven't gotten any more [forms], so that's just where we are for now. They don't do their jobs and we lose revenue" (November 19, 2006). Other managers expressed similar frustration during meetings with principals and parent coordinators, but emphasized that the kids, not United's profits, were suffering. Principals and parent coordinators seemed to agree that the DOE's inability to provide and distribute forms was negatively affecting SES enrollment.

Dispersing enrollment forms at the beginning of each school year is an enormous task— first, for the DOE officials who must determine how many SES packets and in what languages each school should receive, and, second, for the school administration (usually the parent coordinator) who must determine how to get the packets to the eligible students. Since only students that receive free lunch are eligible for services, the school must first determine who gets free lunch.[5] There are often changes from one year to the next, and the final free lunch rosters are not compiled until mid to late October, the same time SES programs are scheduled to begin. Thus, every autumn estimates are made when determining how many forms each school will need, and sometimes enrollment packages are given, by the parent coordinators, to families that do not qualify.

In fall 2006, schools began reporting a shortage of enrollment packets. A few schools reported receiving no SES packets, while others received materials in languages incongruent with their student population. Of the thirty-six schools with which United had partnered that year, nearly two-thirds had not received enough forms, and three had received forms only in Spanish. Parent coordinators distributed enrollment packets based on various criteria, including grade level, test scores, and class number. Such dispersion systems led to parent outcry. Why had a sister's child received a form instead of her child? When would her form be coming? Why was his child not receiving free tutoring? Had her child done something wrong in school to deserve this omission?

Officials cited several reasons for their refusal to supply additional forms, including a previous waste of unlimited forms and the improper distribution by parent coordinators. According to a regional superintendent in Brooklyn, the DOE was merely making the system more efficient. She explained: "We need to get them [parent coordinators] to be mindful of who gets forms and who doesn't. Do you know how many calls I get every day from parents who signed their kids up for SES only to be rejected by us because they don't qualify? If they just gave forms only to free-lunch families, we wouldn't have this problem" (interview, December 7, 2006). Some parent coordinators did, in fact, conserve forms and minimize later DOE rejections of eligibility by giving them only to those families who qualified for free lunch. However, because the free-lunch determinations were not made until after SES enrollment began, some students who qualified did not receive enrollment packets.

Regional superintendents and DOE officials also accused SES providers of seizing forms for their own interests. One explained: "Listen. We know there's a problem. I must've gotten ten calls today from PCs [parent coordinators] asking for more forms, but none of them could explain where missing forms were. I told them if they can give me an explanation for the disappearance, then I'll get them more forms. . . . I can't just be sending more and more forms out there. I don't mean to sound paranoid, but each form represents $2,000 for a provider and we have been told that [SES] providers are out there buying enrollment forms" (interview, December 12, 2006). When I asked for more details, she admitted that the DOE had no evidence that providers were hijacking forms, but added that the DOE was taking the allegations seriously.

The reasons offered by the superintendents seemed implausible. In order for a student to be admitted to an SES program, there were a series of checks and balances in place to ensure that a student not only be eligible, but also that the student had enrolled in only one program. Each enrollment form required a label, which could only be generated by the DOE database, prior to being submitted to an SES provider, so providers could not actually "forge" enrollment forms. Because each enrollment form was processed by the DOE, there could not be duplicates. Reporting attendance was also highly centralized to ensure that SES providers billed only for time attended, in quarter hours.

The DOE's reasons for insufficient enrollments did not make sense to a parent coordinator from a Queens middle school, who, desperate to get forms into the hands of her students, photocopied additional enrollment forms. The school had received enough enrollment packets for only two-thirds of the SES-eligible student population and the demand for packets exceeded the supply. To solve the problem, the parent coordinator distributed full-colored photocopies that were a good likeness for the originals, although the paper stock was unmatched. Two hundred twelve students returned the counterfeit forms, which were submitted to United and accepted by the DOE. As more parent coordinators photocopied counterfeit versions of enrollment forms, parent coordinators and principals were notified by a DOE administrator that photocopies would not be accepted. One SES provider was later reprimanded by the DOE for giving a school photocopied enrollment forms, with their name and provider code handwritten in on the form, a clear violation of SES regulations.

Parent coordinators also asked the DOE for solutions to what one Bronx principal referred to as the "heaping mounds of papers, the overwhelming amount of SES information given to parents." The process, they argued, presented numerous challenges to parents and guardians. In particular, the parents received too much information and too few directives on how to use the information. Some parent coordinators did not give out the complete SES information packets, but instead distilled the main SES points into an SES fact sheet that they distributed. Other coordinators chose not to distribute the packets at all, but invited parents and guardians to SES informational events. At the start of each school year, however, most schools distributed SES information packets, which included a parent notification letter, a brochure, a provider directory that in 2006–7 was a hundred pages long, and a provider selection form. Parents and guardians were also provided with enrollment guides that covered the following sections: frequently asked questions, SES calendar, parent/guardian checklist, questions to ask providers, and list of providers, as well as a provider selection form and instructions on how to complete it. In addition, parents were, in each publication, directed to "visit the website of the New York State Education Department" to get more information.

All the actions parents were to take, according to federal and local authorities, were nearly impossible for most working parents and guardians; even those who wanted particular SES programs to best meet the needs of their children, often did not have the option of choosing it. Although SES was represented in NCLB as a "parent-choice" program, schools, not parents, entered into partnerships with SES providers. Principals decided which providers would offer services at their schools, and parents were directed to enroll only with those providers.

Still, there was a need for local educational agencies to "manage impressions" (Garfinkel 1967)—to appear that in fact, parents were free to choose any SES program.[6] There was also the need for school administrators to present themselves as the experts who knew best. Parents were often told in parent meetings and open houses that they were free to choose an SES provider, but that the school had already found the best programs for their students. During an open school night, the principal of one Queens middle schools introduced the SES providers she had chosen as the most qualified to meet the distinct needs of the schools' student population. She stated: "We have *thoroughly researched* it and these three providers are by far the best to meet your children's needs. They are, without a doubt, the highest qualified to get our test scores up. *All our years of experience* tells us that these three are the *only* three to choose" (field notes November 13, 2007, emphasis added). Ironically, while the school's population was comprised of 42 percent emergent bilinguals, none of the three providers chosen by the principal offered specific curriculum for those students. Still, her strong recommendations went unchallenged by parents, who deferred to her expertise and authority.

Policy is made in many contexts by diverse actors, and SES mandates link an increasing variety of public and private policy mediators, each of whom makes claim to policy authority. School administrators, the DOE, and United Education are observed, in this chapter, to be vying for decision-making power. The ability to affect, if not make, policy is dispersed internally in organizations and schools, as well. In the chapter's last example, a parent coordinator takes matters into her own hands by literally creating simplified SES fact sheets rather than dispersing the official SES materials, and a principal chooses an SES provider that likely cannot adequately serve her students.

In examining the acts of SES selection and other processes of localization in this chapter, multiple, intersecting, and often conflicting practices in appropriating NCLB are revealed. So too are many small acts of defiance in the everyday actions (de Certeau 1984) made obvious. Photocopying enrollment forms when not enough were available; hiring teachers who may not have been skilled enough to teach; and providing inadequate space for students to attend SES, for example, are all somewhat noncompliant in fixing the problem of failure. The actions were all, however, practical and thus necessary actions in appropriating NCLB and attending to failure. Actors constructed their reality through their actions to make sense of their ceaselessly changing circumstances. NCLB steers action toward school failure in a generic manner—i.e., local educational agencies, schools, and SES providers must do something about it—but what exactly they do, is somewhat flexible. Collecting the local agencies, schools, and the tutoring industry together implies a certain regulation of actions. It does not, as demonstrated in this chapter, prohibit the flow of activity in multiple, and nonlinear directions. NCLB directs, but does not determine, action.

FABRICATING FAILURE

Making Up the Need for "Help"

Culturing school failure requires an exaggeration or a misinterpretation, intentional or otherwise, of the signs of failure. It also demands, more often than we may realize, the fabrication of failure—the performing of failure, where none of the accepted markers by which we have come to recognize and name it actually exists. Sometimes, through inaccurate translations and transcriptions, appropriating No Child Left Behind (NCLB) at the district and school levels results in the manufacturing of failure. As federal and state educational policies, and the policy-directed actions of school districts, schools, and supplemental educational service (SES) providers interact, failure is produced rather than found and confronted. In this chapter, I present three examples of inventing failure; the cases involve the actions of many in schools, the Department of Education (DOE), and United Education.

In this chapter's three instances, attending to nonexistent failure, agents of United and the schools create additional "problems" to which they must attend. Tracing NCLB-directed testing and scoring—of standardized state examinations, school-specific tests, and required SES pre- and posttests—across several schools and United Education (Latour's oligopticons) and the DOE's central office and the assessment office of the state's education department (Latour's centers of calculation), the three examples demonstrate the highly variable and selective implementation of NCLB. In each instance, failure is constructed through the actions, not of children, but of the adult policy actors, who are mandated to attend to them.

A United instructor continually directs her seventh-grade students to recite multiplication tables, not because they have yet to master the skill, but rather because "kids at failing schools," according to the instructor, need such recitation to become successful. In this first example, the instructor chooses to ignore the scripted United curriculum in favor of the multiplication tables because, as a retired DOE teacher, she believes she has greater expertise than United. She chooses, I initially believe, not to use the program's pretests to determine what skills the students need to review, but come to learn that in fact, United and its partner school principal do not support using the pretests diagnostically. Again, following the NCLB rules (in this case, pretesting students in SES programs) is more important than what seems commonsensical—using the pretest data diagnostically to customize the curriculum.

In contrast, the third case illustrates how Public School (PS) 100, a school that is misidentified by the DOE as failing, turns it attentions toward improving its (nonexistent) failure by, among other actions, partnering with United. A miscalculation of adequate yearly progress (AYP) places PS 100 on the schools in need of improvement (SINI)list, leading the principal to petition for removal from the list while simultaneously attending to the mock failure at the school. Working with United administrators, the principal organizes the SES classes by ability grouping and sequences the curriculum differently for each grade based on tests given by the school. Beyond adding the SES program, which is required by the school's misplacement on the SINI list, the principal and her staff also determine ways in which they can best tackle their school's erroneous failure.

The second example reveals a United supervisor reporting students' pretest grades as much lower than the actual scores. In essence, he constructs a state of failure for a large number of SES students at PS 80 to ensure greater gains will be seen in the comparative posttests of the program. These tests, which are created, monitored, and scored by each SES provider, and then reported to schools and DOE administrators, are often used to determine the success of particular SES programs. Fearing that PS 80 would not renew United's SES contract if clear gains were not be reported, the supervisor chose to lower the pretest scores, which resulted in a host of additional dilemmas for the supervisor, for United, and for PS 80.

All three instances illustrate what can happen when information is collected and performance is consistently monitored and evaluated under the accountability focus of NCLB. In each case, there is an evaluation, an assessment of policy outcomes. The students, who must recite multiplication tables, are judged as in need of remediation because they are part of the target population of NCLB. The supervisor is judged for the academic progress against measurable criteria (the improvement between pre- and posttest scores) to be made by students in United's SES. PS 100 is judged to be failing by a miscalculation in DOE expectations and indicators that put all schools under annual monitoring. All of these, I argue, are the unintended consequences of NCLB's insistence on "performativity"—"a regime of accountability that employs judgments, comparisons and displays as means of control, attrition and change" (Ball 2008, 49).

Multiplying, Multiplying, and Multiplying, Again

> Six times one is six. Six times two is twelve. Six times three is eighteen. Six times four is twenty-eight. Uh, I mean twenty-four. Six times five is thirty, duh. . . . It's a five times! Five times always end in zeros and fives. . . . We knew this like in first grade or something. (Seventh-grade student in a United SES class, December 8, 2005)

As the student repeats aloud the times table for multiples of six, the SES instructor nods in agreement with each correct product. The next student begins: "Seven times one is seven," and the next is instructed to "do the eights." The nine students each take their turns, with the instructor encouraging them all to do "the tens" in unison. Only one student makes repeated mistakes, giving twenty-six as the product of seven times four and fifty-four as the product of seven times six.

Students who are not reciting the tables are either text-messaging on their cell phones, applying makeup, or working on other homework—i.e., they do not appear engaged with the lesson.[1] One student says aloud that the exercise is for "babies," and a second calls it "so fucking weak." Two others argue that reciting the tables is "like a total waste of time" and "way more stupid than what we do in the day." One student raises her hand to point out that the times tables are not, in fact, part of their lesson, titled "Properties of Operations." The United SES instructor tells her that they must first learn the basics to be "successful in higher mathematics." Another student complains (without raising his hand) that the instructor is treating them like "retards." To this, the instructor directs all the students to recite, in unison, the tens.

The lesson, as written in United's curriculum book, does not include instructions for reciting the multiplication tables, and the students repeatedly demonstrate that they do not need practice—a fact that the students have made clear and that they "discuss" on notes they pass back and forth. One collective note, written alternately by three students, on the lesson page that begins with the instructions "Name the property shown on the line provided," reads,

> *Student 1:* We know this shit.
> *Student 2:* Duh!
> *Student 1:* She [the instructor] must not know it. LOL [Laughing out loud].
> *Student 3:* She's so stupid.
> *Student 1:* She needs it.
> *Student 3:* It?
> *Student 1:* To learn times.
> *Student 3:* No! She don't know what the fuck to teach us.
> *Student 2:* Or how to fucking teach at all (field notes, December 8, 2005)!

The students construct the instructor as a "failure," at doing multiplication tables and at teaching, just as she constructs them as "remedial" learners with regards to multiplication skills. Co-constructing each other in this way overshadows the lesson content and becomes the work that seems to simultaneously engage both the students and the teacher.

Both constructions seem unfounded. The teacher is a retired DOE teacher, who taught mathematics for twenty years in a New York City high school, often lauded at United Education as the best in science and mathematics. She has taught for United's SES program for two years. On two occasions, she was chosen to co-train United SES instructors during a professional development session, entitled "Teaching Students to Overcome Math Phobias."

Among the seven students present for the lesson, five had passed the state examinations with level 3 proficiencies. Another had received the highest mark of level 4. According to their daytime mathematics teachers, all of the students were able to perform mathematics at their grade level. Two of the students were tardy with assignments, and one had lately been missing a class or two per week, but all were passing their mathematics courses, which included geometry and algebra. Further, five of the seven students had taken the United SES pretest and scored, on the average, twenty-three correct out of a total of twenty-five math questions. On the pretest, none had made errors on problems that required (triple-digit) multiplication.

There were no indications that the students needed to recite multiplication tables, and the United seventh-grade curriculum did not include any exercises or lessons on multiplication tables. The instructor was competent to teach higher level mathematics skills, and the students were present to learn them. I asked the instructor about her focus on the multiplication tables. She readily admitted that the multiplication tables were not part of the United lesson, but that she felt "strongly about teaching the basics to these kinds of kids." "These kinds of kids" she defined as ones that go to poor schools in poor neighborhoods and need all the extra help they can get so they don't "fail in life."

After I shared the students' state and United test scores with her, the instructor continued to insist that "drilling the basics" was needed despite what the test scores show. She asserted: "I know what I know. After all these years, I see that kids go up the grades, learning new equations and formulas, but when it comes time to take tests, they blow the easy stuff, like multiplying six times nine. . . . Trust me. I've seen this time and time again" (interview, December 13, 2005). Ignoring the legislated measures of success, highly standardized test scores, the instructor continued to place the high-scoring students in a position of possible, if not eminent, failure. Taking practical actions accepted, if not expected, in a program aimed specifically at ending school failure, the instructor took actions to make sense of her position and the aims of SES, which she situated as "remediation."

When questioned why she didn't focus her instruction on what the students had not known when taking the United pretest rather than what they had demonstrated they knew, like multiplication tables, the instructor informed me that she never saw the pretest scores. She thought that she would see the overall scores when midterm progress reports were sent home from United, but that she still would not know in what areas the students had difficulty. This was confirmed by United's SES director. According to him, United pretests and midterm tests were not diagnostic, and their results were not intended to inform instruction. What then, I asked, did the tests inform? The director replied: "To measure how we're doing. . . . The DOE requires we do quarterly progress reports and parents like when we include test scores. . . . Numbers or scores matter to parents." The tests, which could have been a curriculum guiding tool for instructors, were instead used as props that allowed United to appear as if they were measuring—and by logical extension attending to—the students' specific skill weaknesses. They weren't. Although United had the data, they did not have the academic expertise or support to use it to differentiate instruction. They used it only for reporting purposes as required by NCLB.

While collecting the data fulfilled United's contract with the DOE, which required progress to be tracked, recorded, and reported, it also served United's contractual duty to demonstrate its ability to increase student achievement. According to NCLB, providers that failed to show (with their own data) that they could increase achievement scores within two years were to lose their state approval to provide SES. One United manager explained this to the principal at Junior High School (JHS) 345. He stated that the test scores indicated how well United was testing, not how well students were performing. The principal replied that she "would be the one to grade United's performance" and would look closely at "the end-of-the-year [United] progress report," which included the pre-, mid-, and posttest scores, along with the average percentile changes in mathematics and English language arts (ELA) by grade level. In an interview, the principal stated that United's test scores, along with state assessment grades, would determine whether or not she invited United back for the next year.

In the same interview, however, she stated that what really mattered to her was that United was doing the tests. She explained:

I need the SES providers to do their jobs. If they say they're going to do something, they better damn well do it. Like the pre, pre, post, mid, whatever tests they say they do. They better just do them. And then they better tell me how it went. If they don't, I just don't return their calls or ask them back. They let me down—and that matters more to me really than the scores. Scores go up and down. . . . I want to see results, but I really want to see effort. (interview, March 15, 2006)

The assistant principal, in a separate interview, confirmed that performing the tests was as important, if not more important, than the actual results. She said, "Well, it's really about doing the tests. We need to do the tests repeatedly, again and again, so that kids and parents see we are serious about this testing stuff. . . . When the providers give tests or practice tests it's like one more time. . . . And the scores, well we need the numbers, God knows, especially this year since we went down last year, but what we really need is the testing. Parents are always asking about testing. They actually want more testing" (interview, May 10, 2006). Initially, I was skeptical that parents wanted more testing, but this was confirmed by a DOE parent survey (2006). The importance of testing for the school administration seemed to be twofold: They wanted the SES providers, like United, to administer the three tests as promised (and required by NCLB) and then they also wanted parents to know that the school administration was supportive of testing their children throughout the day and also in the afterschool programs.

The 2005–6 and 2006–7 United progress reports for JHS 345, the parts of which the principal directly downloaded into her own annual school reports, showed 5–7 percent increases in United's SES test scores across all grades in ELA, but varied from 5 percent increases to 11 percent decreases in mathematics. Such fluctuations were common, but United's SES managers were instructed by the director to "play up the reports as an invaluable service" even though the reports, including the results of the three tests given during United's SES program, often indicated a reduction in test scores. Internal marketing instructions stated, "Be sure to tell parents that we give three tests, a pretest to see where their child is, a midterm test to prepare their child for the state examinations, and a posttest to measure progress." Thus, the actions of giving the tests and reporting the results were given importance at United over the actual scores. Even though some scores indicated failure and others demonstrated success by NCLB standards, all scores were secondary to the actions—testing and reporting scores—which was seen as attending to failure. This resonated with JHS 345's priority, as well, and the principal invited United back into the school for three continuous years.

Similarly, the teaching of the United instructor, who insisted on having students recite the multiplication tables, was judged more important than her lessons' content. The instructor's performance had been observed annually by United trainers. From reviewing the performance observations, I learned that she was "an excellent teacher with great command of the classroom" and "a truly gifted teacher." I also saw, however, that she "failed to teach the lesson material," "didn't follow the United lesson," and "stayed off topic too long." Nonetheless, she received the highest mark of "exemplary display" in all categories, including "knows lesson content" and "follows structure of the lesson page." Again, performing the action seemed to take precedence over the results of the action.

Providing lessons and giving examinations were perceived as normative requirements for the pragmatic action of attending to school failure. The activities were contingent upon the practicality of the circumstance. The instructor was doing what needed to be done not for failing children, but to meet the no-nonsense expectation of accountability set in NCLB. Conflict between the stated goal of eliminating failure by improving test scores and the acts of drilling students on the basics and giving practice examinations was nearly invisible in the daily work of United.

Rescoring Examinations

In the spring of 2008, SES pretest scores, which seemed to indicate students' proficiency and measured success in ELA, were purposefully lowered by a United staff member at a Staten Island elementary school. Fearing that the "high" pretest scores would make it impossible for the program to show improvement, a program supervisor chose not to report the actual pretest scores of nearly sixty students, who had scored greater than 80 percent, but rather to record manufactured scores of less than 50 percent. After collecting the score sheets from the instructors, he manipulated the test score sheets to reflect the new failing scores, which were entered into the SES division's database by a part-time office employee unaware of the falsification. He prioritized United's "survival" over the interests of the students.

In keeping with the principal's directives, students were grouped into SES classes according to proficiency, as indicated by pretest scores. According to the principal, "Tracking, I mean grouping, students by ability level helps us focus on the things they don't know by class, rather than by student. My teachers work all day and I don't need them having to figure out who knows what every SES lesson with the ELA tests coming up so soon." However, unbeknownst to the principal, the tests of nearly sixty students had been misreported, and thus classes were essentially mixed in level.

The scores went unquestioned until the second month of the program when quarterly student progress reports, which included the arbitrarily manufactured scores, were sent home to parents and guardians. Again, it should be noted that according to United's practice, within NCLB requirements, and as discussed in the previous example, the scores were not explicitly shared with SES instructors or students immediately after the examination. So, it was not a student, an instructor, nor a United manager, but a parent who first questioned her son's pretest score of 40 percent. Her inquiry was quickly followed by five others—and a United office employee, responsible for hearing the concerns on the parent hotline, notified a manager of the parents' concerns about test scores at the school.

By the time I first learned about what parents were calling "misreported" and "impossible" scores, the manager had reviewed the answer sheets for all 228 tests taken at the Staten Island school and had found seventy-two sheets to contain, in his words, an "excessive combination of erasure marks, changed answers, and illegible marks." My interview with the manager took place the week after his review of the test scores. When I asked about the test scores, the manager responded:

> You heard? No shit? The parents talked to you about the tests? Never mind. It doesn't matter. I'll tell you, there's a problem. I mean, I can tell you that I think there's a problem, but I don't know for sure yet. It's really screwed up at that school. There are all these tests, seventy-something, that seem suspicious, like they were changed or something. I have to find out whether or not they were changed after the fact or if kids were given the right answers during the test or what. . . . What's really weird, most of the changed answers are wrong not right like I'd expect. Who the hell would give kids the wrong answers? It doesn't make any sense. (interview February 29, 2008)

The manager was right. The situation didn't make sense as long as he focused his explanation on what children had likely done—adjusted their score sheets after being given answers—rather than what adults, or in this case, one adult, may have done.

Two weeks later, I learned from an SES instructor that one of the program supervisors had confessed to changing the scores and had been terminated by the manager. According to the fired supervisor, he had lowered the scores—in effect, manufactured failure—because he wanted the posttest scores to show a "huge measurable improvement." He stated,

> It's like in order for us, I mean them [United Education] to keep up their ac-counts, they need to show that we're doing something. You know, like we're making kids learn. . . . The principal kept saying that we had to improve test scores or else we wouldn't be back next year. . . . I shouldn't have changed the scores. It was stupid. . . . The kids did really well and I screwed it up and made it look like they didn't. . . . I didn't think anyone would know and that they'd all be really happy when the scores went up at the end. (interview, April 4, 2008)

The manager confirmed that the school's principal had, in fact, been very "score focused" and adamant about United Education improving test scores, but he did not explicitly correlate the principal's behaviors with the supervisor's acts.

What to make of the misreported scores became central to the SES administrators. A series of e-mails, phone calls, and statements ensued; the following excerpts demonstrate how the supervisor's actions set into motion a flurry of activity at United.

E-mail from SES manager to SES director, dated March 3, 2008:

> . . . so we have a problem. The test scores at PS 80 were changed by the site supervisor. I found [out] yesterday after bringing the issue up with all the su-pervisors and teachers. After the meeting, he told me that he did it. Trouble is that he doesn't know which ones he changed. He says he changed sixty of them, but like I told you, I found more than seventy to be questionable. Can we meet in the morning?

Response, the same evening:

> Yes, we must meet. 8 am in my office.

During the meeting, the SES director called one of United's lawyers for advice and was told not to do anything but get the facts. As the manager recounted this to me, he shook his head, saying that at that meeting, he had no idea what trouble had been created.

I was not invited to attend any of the follow-up meetings and became aware of United's explanation of test discrepancies when PS 80's principal showed me an e-mail she had received from the SES director. In part, it read, "An error in our database rendered some of the ELA pretests taken in our SES program invalid. . . . We have begun retesting all of the students. . . . Our system has been since remedied and we have begun retesting students. As scoring the examinations are a priority, we will complete the process by early next week and set up a time to meet with you again" (personal communication March 8, 2008). The principal assured me that the "situation" had been taken care of and that she and the director had already met. She praised him for his prompt actions in contacting her, but remained somewhat skeptical about United's ability to get reliable scores through retesting. She noted: "It will be impossible for them to get the same scores on the tests again. For one thing the kids have been in the program for a month and they have already seen the test. . . . We don't have another option and I'm scared. I used those test scores as a marker to see how we were doing. Now, for all I know, kids are doing much worse. The scores could be elevated (interview, April 3, 2008). Apparently, the nature of the misreported scores was not explained to the principal, and although she had been very unyielding about grouping students by ability, the principal did not argue when classes were not regrouped using the new test scores.

Fabricating low test scores speaks to the inherent double paradox for SES providers. For SES providers to demonstrate that their afterschool programs increase academic performance—i.e., reduce failure—they must first have low achievement to address. Because children enrolled in SES are not necessarily the ones who did not score well on the state examinations (by which AYP is calculated), they may demonstrate proficiency on pretests. Further, if providers like United do, in fact, demonstrate improvement and contribute to improved state test scores, they essentially work themselves out of employment. The PS 80 principal, operating under NCLB sanctions, required explicit proof of SES's efficacy. Her demands were translated, perhaps mistranslated, into the need for demonstrated increases between SES pre- and posttests—and the supervisor, through his actions, made possible the room for measured improvement. He constructed failure so that success could be more easily demonstrated.

Failing an Outstanding School

By multiple measures—those that are standardized and those that are not—PS 100, in general, was exceptional. The school's mission statement told us that they honored, among other things, hard work, effort, cooperation, kindness, honesty, generosity, and responsibility (New York City DOE, 2006).[2] The principal's statement explained to us that the staff passionately believed that children learn best when they are given chances to play, sing, think, question, socialize, explore, build, and work hard. The principal, who enjoyed widespread support and respect from PS 100 teachers, staff, and parents, was seen by United's field manager as "the exception to the rule in public education—someone who believed that learning could be transformative." The principal was quick to point out that learning is important for everyone, and she encouraged her staff to learn something new every day and to teach it to someone else. The school's policies and educating practices consistently reflected these values—and by all accountabilities under NCLB, PS 100 was a success.

The 576 students at PS 100 attend pre-kindergarten through fifth-grade classes, in which the average class size is less than twenty-three students. The school, when it came under study in 2005, was at 74.5 percent capacity, boasted a 92.3 percent attendance rate, and a student stability rate of 95.2 percent. During the 2004–5 school year, all forty-eight teachers were fully licensed and permanently assigned to the school, an increase of 4.4 percent from the 2003–4 academic year. Greater than one-half of the money at PS 100 was spent on classroom instruction.

In addition to classroom instruction, the school promoted multiple additional programs. PS 100 had partnerships with multiple New York City organizations, including Teachers College, Arts Connection, Carnegie Hall, Lincoln Center, the local YMCA, and the Metropolitan Opera. Extracurricular activities included literacy support and lunchtime sports intramurals and enrichment clusters in chess, technology, and debate. The parent-teacher association (PTA) supported various programs for parents and families and had secured several grants to fund parent workshops, including English as a second language courses.

What is most notable, however, is that PS 100 was a barrier-free site with full integration of on-site services, inclusion classes, and self-contained classes for the 136 students categorized by the New York City DOE as special education students and English language learners. Prior to the school's official start time, groups of students in wheelchairs and walkers participated in an exercise/motion class in the cafeteria. Throughout the day, individual students—some with lowered visibility or hearing or mobility—were assisted in the classrooms, the lunchroom, and on the playground. Spanish was heard throughout the halls, the administrative offices, and the outside school grounds. After they had brought their children to learn, some parents stayed for English classes sponsored by the school. PS 100 appeared well integrated at a time when some principals were trying to reduce their number of special education students, who according to a principal at a nearby grade school "bring down the numbers and keep us from meeting our AYPs."

At PS 100 it was not the inclusion of special education students and English language learners that kept them from meeting their AYP requirement. It was rather, the DOE's failure to include the scores of these particular subsets of PS 100 students in the calculations. Without the scores of the fourth-grade special education students and English language learners, who were given additional provisions during testing and therefore took the tests separately from the rest of their fourth-grade peers, it was made to appear that less than 95 percent of the fourth graders actually took the ELA examination. So, although the students' scores were well above the benchmark set for their demographic groups, they were not added to the school's total AYP calculation for the ELA test—and thus the school failed to meet the ELA goal, which like all AYP goals, requires that at least 95 percent of the fourth graders take the examination. Since English language learners were not tested separately in math and science, their scores were included and PS 100 met AYP requirements in those two areas.

In the year 2005–6, the state's education department and the DOE realized the mistake, essentially a mathematical error and the regional superintendent petitioned to put a hold on PS 100's official status. Nonetheless, PS 100 was placed on the SINI list and was subjected to all the requirements of SINI schools, including offering SES. The principal and the superintendent verbally petitioned and wrote letters of petition to School Chancellor Joel Klein. In 2006–7, the state removed PS 100 from the list of failing schools, but New York City's DOE did not. The principal petitioned again.

Being (mis)assigned to the list created a series of "problems" that required action on behalf of the principal, the teachers, the parents, the students, and the school's SES provider, United Education. The greatest responsibility fell to the principal, who repeatedly explained the mistake to parents, teachers, and United mangers as she continued to petition for a change of status. Because PS 100 was officially assigned to the failing schools list, the students were technically eligible for SES. However, because the school was, in fact, meeting its AYP goals, the principal was ironically required, each year, to apply for "special condition" permission from the city's DOE to have SES programs.

A conversation at a teachers' autumn 2006 staff meeting exemplifies the difficulties faced by the principal. After explaining the miscalculation that placed PS 100 on the SINI list for the second year, the principal asks for questions.

> *Teacher 1 (T1):* We are a successful SINI that is failing?
>
> *Teacher 2 (T2):* Or are we a failing SINI because we are succeeding, excelling? [laughter throughout room]
>
> *T1:* Face it. We're succeeding and the DOE thinks we're failures.
>
> *Principal (P):* Actually, they [the DOE] know we met our AYP last year and this year.
>
> *Teacher 3 (T3):* So, why are we SINI again?
>
> *T2:* Because the DOE can't imagine that a school with so many immigrants and Special Education students could actually not fail by their standards.
>
> *T1:* Yea, kind of like that.
>
> *P:* I'm frustrated too! We are a remarkable success here. All of you know that. I certainly know that. They [the DOE] say we need improvement because we failed to meet the ELA AYP, but we didn't. . . . I don't want us to get hung up on labels. We know that we met the AYP and still we need to direct some energy into all the things that get thrown at us for being a SINI. We know how to do this, even if we don't want to, right?
>
> *T1:* But who are we failing in comparison to? We are a school in need of improvement? Have you looked around lately? Look at PS 200. Now that's failure. (field notes September 18, 2006)

The PS 100 teachers struggled to find a lexicon with which to talk about their school's status and ultimately agreed that PS 100 was a successful school that had, in the words of a veteran teacher (T3), "just been branded with the failure label."

Nonetheless, for the next half hour, teachers worked to make sense of the SINI designation. The teachers focused on how to attend to the failure, which the students were not, in the aggregate, demonstrating. They decided to have the students do more concentrated vocabulary and arithmetic in small groups; to tutor individual students for a larger part of each day; and to make weekly benchmarks for their classes to meet. They were, as a group, addressing the failure as if they had not succeeded. In order to make some sense of their school's placement on the failing schools list, they focused on fixing the "failure." They would "perform" attending to failure and would "pass" as a "failing school," only so their success could ultimately be irrefutable.

The twelve United teachers and two supervisors also addressed the success/failure standing of PS 100. During the preprogram training, the lead supervisor explained the miscalculation that resulted in the school's SINI status. She reported: "Since this school isn't really failing, we will be working with children who may or may not need our program. Most of them probably didn't fail their exams, but it's still good for us to do preventative reinforcement of skills. . . . And really, there must be other reasons why we're here. I mean they aren't totally successful school or we wouldn't be here" (field notes, October 25, 2006). The United teachers agreed and on two separate occasions in November 2006 repeated similar ideas to the students, who were between eight and ten years old. One United teacher told his class: "You aren't failures. You're the best. We just want you to be even better. Everyone can do better. Each of you can score higher and higher and higher on your tests." Another teacher told her students to consider United, "the cherry on top of the ice cream sundae—an extra special treat, the best part." And so went the discourse to explain why so many people, including PS 100 and United teachers, were orienting themselves to the students' failure that didn't actually exist.

Notably, in the autumn of 2006, only 103 students, thirty-eight less than the previous year, were enrolled for United Education tutoring. When asked about the decline in SES enrollments, the parent coordinator explained that once she was sure the school had been *mistakenly* put on the SINI list, there was less urgency to sign students up for tutoring. In fact, she continued, she had done less to advertise the program and had asked United not to hand out informational flyers to parents at arrival and dismissal times. The United manager concurred: "It's kinda rough trying to sell a remedy for failure to parents whose kids aren't failing." However, when asked why PS 100 even had an on-site tutoring program, both the parent coordinator and the SES manager said that it was added insurance for next year's tests—i.e., a preventative activity.

In addition to offering SES, an NCLB requirement, there were other consequences of being on the SINI list. For instance, because PS 100 had "made" the SINI list, students from other failing schools could not choose to attend PS 100 under the public school choice option. As a result, PS 100s classes remained, on the average, below twenty-three students, and the total enrollment remained slightly below 75 percent capacity while other schools were well over 100 percent. The smaller classes were welcomed by parents and teachers.

A member of the PTA cited the small class sizes as the main reason she would not remove her child from the school, even though she had once considered putting her son in a nearby Catholic school. Another parent, who volunteered at the school, described the small class size as "a gift to her daughter, her family, and the wonderful teachers [at PS 100]." The PTA secretary said that everyone was thankful for the SINI status for keeping "all the white, upper-middle class parents from choosing PS 100 and turning it into a South PS 300"—a reference to the "successful" PS 300 located two-miles north of PS 100, so highly sought after that parents have been known to stand outside overnight to be the first in line on enrollment day.

The parents' sentiments were echoed by a veteran teacher, who had taught at two overcrowded grade schools before transferring to PS 100, but five newer teachers, each in their fourth year of teaching, had never taught in an overcrowded classroom. They were each highly sought after by a number of districts and individual schools across the state once they had received stellar marks for their student teaching—and all chose PS 100 from a list of failing schools. Although not a publicized program, a local DOE administrator explained the "informal practice of getting the best teachers to the students and schools who need them most"—i.e., the failing schools. She said that first they tried to place experienced teachers in SINI schools, but that quality new teachers are the "next best thing." The superintendent described how she placed the highest quality student teachers at those schools in the district that had the greatest chance of getting off the SINI list without corrective action. The procedure had worked, she said. When questioned about placing such teachers at PS 100, a school that actually wasn't failing, she quickly answered: "Well, of course they aren't technically failing, but they are indeed on the list . . . and these young people [the newly certified teachers] want to feel like they are making a difference. So everyone wins in some way. They succeed and PS 100 gets to keep working on getting off the SINI list. . . . It doesn't add to their problems" (interview, August 24, 2006). So again, another person, in this case, a regional administrator, was orienting herself and her practices toward failure, toward the "problems" at PS 100, while simultaneously acknowledging that failure had not actually occurred.

Most of those associated with PS 100, including the principal, the regional superintendent, and many teachers believed that by the beginning of the 2007–8 school year, PS 100 would no longer be a SINI school. Being removed from the list, in fact, was a high priority for the principal. She not only contacted her superiors and officials at the DOE, but devoted the largest section in her comprehensive educational plan to the removal. In notable contrast, the parent coordinator expressed no optimism that all the efforts of the administration, the staff, the parents, or the teachers would change the school's status. She reasoned, "Failure is the Scarlet S [or perhaps, 'F']. Once you get it, you wear it and can't get away from it. It becomes this glaring situation that needs attention." Given the ways in which addressing the arbitrarily assigned failure had become so prominent at PS 100 during 2005 and 2006, both stances seem understandable and either outcome a likely possibility.

In spring 2007, the school was removed from the SINI list. They were no longer seen as a "failing" school. However, their newly acknowledged success brought with it two new problems related to afterschool tutoring. First, the school was no longer eligible for SES but still had students enrolled in United's program, which was not yet finished for the year. Second, the parents began demanding that the tutoring program continue since it had "gotten our school off the list." To solve the first problem, the principal petitioned the director of SES in New York City, and the students who were already enrolled in the program were allowed to finish the program.

Addressing the second problem, which was seemingly based on the misconception that the school had been failing but with the help of United tutoring had improved to a successful status, proved more difficult and expensive to resolve. After holding a series of parent meetings to explain that the tutoring, while helpful, did not directly result in the school's removal from the SINI list, the principal acquiesced to the parents' requests for a continued afterschool tutoring program. Since the school was not SES eligible, the principal had to develop her own afterschool enhancement program and hire her teachers to tutor the students. The principal bought a set of United curriculum often purchased by schools for test-taking support, but was not as pleased with it as she had been with the curriculum used in the United SES program.[3]

When asked about the school's enhancement program, the principal explained:

> I was afraid this would happen. Once we were marked as failing, everyone here, well almost everyone started working on the failure that wasn't really there. It was like we were all taking care of a failing school, but we weren't obviously failing. We were marked a SINI school and then we got this sort of limp and started limping along. So then we got the crutches—you know, SES and PD (professional development) and some coaching from the region—and now we still limp. . . . I don't know why any of us started limping, but we did and now we'll have to rehab. (interview September 27, 2007)

The parent coordinator concurred. In a separate interview, she summarized:

> Honestly, I'm surprised parents complained. Fewer signed up and really, I thought that we had done a good job of letting parents know that we were never really failing. . . . I'm actually shocked that we got off the list. Maybe parents are too and it'll just take a while for them to get used to this new thing. You know, success being recognized as success instead of failure. . . . They're just used to the free tutoring and the additional help. They'll learn to do without it because the kids don't need it. (October 12, 2007)

Other staff members also suggested that in the near future the parents would stop missing the SES program, quit worrying about failure, and become happy that their children went to a successful school.

Members of the PTA at PS 100 disagreed. The secretary, who had not enrolled her child in the SES program, warned:

> Lots of parents here work two or three jobs. Both parents, usually. So, having their kids in a safe educational environment allowed them more flexible and longer work schedules. By putting their kids in SES, they were able to pick them up at 5:30 instead of 3:30 and that's got to be a big difference in work hours. Most of our parents are Mexican immigrants who want their children to succeed. So, you know they do what they think will help their kids. Like work more hours to provide for them and put them in tutoring. . . . Parents

aren't going to stop this just because the school got off some list it was never on. Hey, if I had to work, I'd put Alyssa in SES too. (interview, October 26, 2007)

Two other PTA officers, who had enrolled their children in the SES program, agreed with the secretary that parents will do what they think is best for their children or for their families. Several parents, who had enrolled their children in United's program in the two previous years, contacted United directly asking why the company was no longer providing services at PS 100.

PS 100 is a school that succeeded, met its AYP goals, but was still designated by some miscalculation made at a "center of calculation" as failing for up to three years beyond what is warranted by calculation. It became framed by the misdesignation of "failing school," and those associated with the school—the administrators, the staff, the teachers, the parents, and the students—became engaged in the highly patterned and ritualized behaviors and cultural activities that underlie, organize, and often conserve school "failure." The United staff, called in to provide some insurance against future failure, also took actions to ward off the "problem." Most were working hard, orienting themselves to the failure that had mistakenly overtaken them.

Many were attending to the failure not necessarily of any individual students or particular groups of students, but to what had been facted through (mis)translation. These agents—principals, parent coordinators, SES providers, government officials—with their complex and social intentional actions and practices, were participating in culturally organized and constructed processes that made failure matter. The intentionality and agency of these individuals in relation to the school failure at (not "of") PS 100 can be recast into the larger cultural and social forces of the American public school system, with its ready-made reforms.

In fact and practice, as seen at PS 100, success and failure define each other and exist only together. They are correlative terms like "health and disease" and "justice and injustice"—"joined terms that rise and fall as a pair, that are clarified and obfuscated together; dealing with one is tantamount to dealing with the other" (Margalit 2002, 112). The fabrication and maintenance of failure requires a thoroughly interdependent matrix, a web wherein failure has meaning by virtue of its relation to the other term in the correlative pair, success. Saussure (1983) points out that meaning is not found in the words themselves, but in the intervals, the contrasts, and the participation between the terms. Teachers and parents and United staff struggled to make sense of their placement on the SINI list and all the problems that came with attending to the failure that did not exist on its own.

Success, a possibility to which we are all to strive, became at PS 100 overshadowed by its counterpart, failure. Even when all the recognized signs of success were apparent, the misreading of them erroneously rendered their measured success illegitimate. Their success became hidden, so to speak because only legitimately identified success stood as the mark by which failure was measured—and, in the predicament of PS 100, mismeasured. Still, the fact that many involved with PS 100 oriented themselves to addressing failure as if the students had, indeed, failed the state examinations, demonstrated the hold that failure, once (mis)constructed as a social fact, exerts over even those who were not failing.

When PS 100 was first designated as failing, there existed "a quantum-moment of instability of meaning . . . of fertile ambiguity pregnant with possibilities and with anxiety" (Taddei 2005, 101). During this moment, the staff at PS 100 began perceiving the characteristics of the situation as being, even if erroneously, a failing school. As their actions materialized into sets of activities directed toward the problem, they began to act as they had been perceived. Never independent of how they had been categorized by the DOE, PS 100 did what it could do to make sense of its designation.

PS 80, PS 100, and JHS 345, along with United, were, indeed, attending to the problem by performing the actions that were recognized, mostly by the parents, as those that needed to be taken. At JHS 345, actions were taken to downplay the uncertainty and lack of predictability in school failure. Nuances were ignored. Students were taught and retaught the basics, and tests were given just to comply with expectations that something be done for students in failing schools. What makes the PS 100 case so remarkable is that the school was not failing. The staff and parents had to work hard to make sense of their designation by taking actions that were in line with the expectations set forth in NCLB.

That failure was made to matter for some students at PS 80, and at all at PS 100, confirms that we do not need failing students or failing groups of students at which to direct attentions. At PS 100, there were students who scored below the norm on the standard tests, but their scores did not directly cause PS 100 to be placed on the SINI list. Still, attending to school failure became a continuous flow of situated practices across multiple and various settings—and agent's engagement with failure made them neither solely compliant nor oppositional to the cultural facting of failure.

The historically constituted setting of the school, which was taken for granted by the agents, informed the choices they made. Most were just doing what they had been trained to do in an educational system that long ago situated success and failure as natural. NCLB reinforced, if not legitimized, the actions even when the need for such action was questionable. The actors at PS 100 were working hard with what was given, what was made or facted for them, and they were never independent of the ways in which other actors in the network constructed and expressed interpretations of them (Varenne, Goldman, and McDermott 1998, 12).

ABANDONING FAILURE

Diffusing Its Impact

Throughout this book, actor-network theory illuminated the interconnectivity of material objects, human actors, and their environments. It displayed the process of mutual shaping; actors worked on their environments and the environments influenced them, in turn. The actor-network emerged when the multiple actions of those attending to school failure flowed from one location to many others. It was always, from its inception, a dynamic, network—expanding as ambiguous boundaries were contested, adjusting as linkages were developed and dissolved, and compromising as deadlines went unmet and participants constructed new aims. I revisit the network now, not as an end product or an explanation, but as a way to talk, again, about how many people worked hard at making failure pay in the situations afforded by No Child Left Behind (NCLB), the federal policy turned law, aimed at eliminating it.

NCLB mandates and directives imply that school failure would be remedied if people would act according to the policy;

as seen in this study, many did act on the policy's 588 regulations. Most "followed" some version of an already extracted and adapted account of the actual regulations to "do" their work. Behaviors varied as actors made sense of what actions they were to take and how they were to take them, according to the partially localized forms and their particular circumstances. Appropriating NCLB went well beyond implementing, or conversely rejecting, a prescribed plan. Policy stakeholders actively apprehended the policy and their circumstances according to the mandates. Contextualizing their actions, actors constructed and engaged in multidirectional schemes of action. They acted not in isolation, but in relation to other actors and to environments. Through these linkages, they made sense of their "call to action" under NCLB, and their practices became structured by the contexts within which they worked.

Patterns of behavior under NCLB emerged, unfolding in the present and being performed through current interactions, in ever-changing situations, but they were grounded within the past and informed by previous interactions (Spillane, Gomez, and Mesler 2009). On multiple levels, the contested history of NCLB (as the long-standing Elementary and Secondary Education Act), the actors' consciousness of the impact of previous federal, state, and local educational policies on schooling, and the record of private-public relationships within education affected the appropriation of the supplemental educational service (SES) mandates. Embedded in every interaction, in every activity, remnants, and memories of remnants, of previous policy conditions, enactments, and consequences were incorporated into the more current implementation of NCLB. As shown, repeatedly, in *Making Failure Pay*, federally allocated change, legitimized by policy, "never eradicates the past in its attempts to craft the future. Policy makers' grand designs do not play out on blank slates, rather they are layered on and entangled in current ways of doing things" (Spillane, Gomez, and Mesler 2009, 411).

Federal and state mandates develop and achieve salience through specific discourses and actions adopted by local entities. Localized policy activities and the "circumstances of local practice are intimately connected to how local actors encounter and perceive the policy directives of federal and state agencies (Spillane, Gomez, and Mesler 2009, 409). The relationships between specific policy directives and exacting policy outcomes under NCLB manifest in critical local policy configurations. They are a "product of an array of factors (many of them unplanned or the consequences of prior policies beyond the education sector) that are difficult to nudge let alone control from the halls of congress or even the statehouse" (411). Through localized processes and practices, the SES mandates of NCLB in this study got implemented in a multiple of divergent ways.

Challenges to NCLB were narrowly orchestrated and focused. Localized contestations by state, district, and local educational agencies, schools, and individuals, such as principals within schools, confronted their interpretations of their roles according to the federal policy, as well as the possibility of meeting the policy's goals given their particular situations. Most human actors in the study did not question the problem at which the policy target—school failure, nor did they challenge NCLB's reliance on a cultural pattern that has long linked academic achievement undisputedly to economics and national well-being. As Smith (2004) recognized, most policy actors take such patterns for granted so that "legislators organize their rule making as if the pattern were real. Courts organize their interpretation of rules as if the pattern were real" (37), and, I would add, that businesses and schools organize their enactment of the rules as if the pattern were not only real, but without competing alternatives. Although the ways in which the policy framed failure determined the preferred solutions, advanced certain actions, and set the course for the implementation of the mandates, few actors challenged the problem.

It was the work—the localized mediation, translation, and constructions of facts—directed at school failure that has been followed in this study. The work moved across institutional and organizational boundaries—through "thing-like" entities, such as educational policy, departments and agencies of education, educational research, and private tutoring and testing companies—and also through activities, including processing test scores, ranking students, and customizing SES programs. There were no clear partitions or impenetrable borders; actors' activities unfolded across multiple settings and circumstances in organizations that were themselves in constant fluctuation.

The complexities in which school failure was embedded were opened to inspection. My research deployed and collected associations; it defragmented and examined the webs of relations. Rather than settle any given controversy, the task was to trace connections between the contradictory and transient group formation and membership. In fact, some patterns among the relationships between schools, SES providers, and NCLB were revealed. My challenge now is to reassemble the fragments—the individual linkages, work, and relationships—that I have argued comprise a particular network, or more literally a "work-net" (Latour 2005, 143). I undertake what Latour (2005) calls "explicitly engaging in the reassembling of the collective" (247).

At first, and until very recently, I attempted to reassemble the examined fragments into a visual map—a tangible network. Each effort either resulted in a diagram with clear entities, such as schools and SES providers, interconnected with a variety of lines (broken, dashed, dotted, and bolded) or overlapping shapes. Each tended toward a "privileged mode of organization" (Latour 2005, 129). Every map gave the impression of a multifaceted, interconnected structure with interchangeable parts or entities. But entities in this study did things; they were not placeholders nor were they interchangeable. Actions were not merely carried through entities. Actors, which were not substitutable, made differences with their actions. Each was a unique actant, totally irreducible to any other (except when rendered by a third actor as commensurable with another by some process of standardization). And the actors, whose work I followed, did not, of course, represent an exhaustive list of actants as portrayed in my attempted diagrams.

Again, I turned to Latour (1993), whose work reminded me that network is a concept, not a thing. He explains:

> Surely you'd agree that drawing *with* a pencil is not the same thing as drawing the *shape* of the pencil. It's the same with this ambiguous word: network. With actor-network you may describe something that doesn't at all look like a network—an individual state of mind, a piece of machinery, a fictional character; conversely, you may describe a network—subways, sewages, telephones—which is not all drawn in an "actor-network" way. You are simply confusing the object with the method. ANT [actor-network theory] is a method, and mostly a negative one at that; it says nothing about the shape of what is being described with it. (142)

The actor-network traced in this study describes multiple actions directed toward school failure. The network is not the "object" being described.

I reassemble the fragments of the network now—again by focusing on the flow of work—to summarize the study's findings. I begin with NCLB, which is, in fact, somewhat of a middle, *in media res,* of the network. In this book, NCLB has been described as both an entity and also a set of interrelated processes. Social relations or associations emerged when NCLB was appropriated. Some were temporary, such as those forged between the staff of SES providers and administrators, teachers, and staffs of particular schools. Various agents transported, mediated, and translated ideas, materials, and services through these associations. The movement of this policy work from one of these associations to the next was maintained, suspended, resumed, and reconfigured by human actors employed by the SES providers and the Department of Education (DOE)—and sometimes working simultaneously for both.

Some NCLB-directed relations lasted longer. The contracts between the state and local educational agencies and SES providers, including United Education, for instance, surpassed for obvious reasons the more temporary associations between United and individual schools. There existed an ongoing bilateral stream of people, papers, and payments between United and agencies of the DOE. The DOE was the client; the SES providers were vendors who needed to be in compliance with DOE regulations. Many actions of the SES providers—hiring teachers, fingerprinting employees, permitting programs, ordering snacks, obtaining security, among others—were highly regulated by DOE employees and offices. Every report—initial student plans, student progress letters, summative reports, pretest and posttest scores, class rosters, emergency contact forms, for example—generated by United and delivered to schools, students, and parents were also submitted to the DOE for approval, and thus, ultimately payment based on compliance.

More enduring associations exist between the federal Education Department (ED), the New York State Education Department (NYSED), and New York City's DOE. Other linkages, which were not directly addressed in this research, continue even longer. NCLB, DOEs, and schools of education, where teachers are trained, curriculum is developed, and critiques of education are generated, have long associations. Tutoring and testing companies that entered the SES market after the passing of NCLB also sustain relationships with schools of education and research institutions. They have long created customized curriculum and tests by selectively drawing upon the work done in academia. Companies like United regularly provide schools, those that receive SES and those that do not, with curriculum, test preparation, teacher coaching, and professional development.

I return to the linkages with NCLB to review the movement of work. Principals of failing schools had to do something about NCLB mandates. The directives of the legislation were inescapable. Among other actions, they were required to offer SES—i.e., they were obliged to partner with at least one SES provider and to offer SES at their schools. Principals were required to spend up to 20 percent of their Title I funds and to provide implementation support to SES programs. As shown, however, the administrators met their responsibility to SES in a number of dissimilar and distinct ways. Some aimed to get as many students enrolled in SES as can be accommodated; others set enrollment limits and reduced marketing opportunities for providers. Since gaining responsibility for their budgets in 2007, some principals chose to begin their own afterschool programs, which competed directly with SES for enrollments.

The actions and inactions of principals set in motion the conduct of many other school employees. When, for example, a principal chose to promote a robust SES program or programs, she appointed an SES contact, usually an assistant principal, dean, or parent coordinator. These administrators were not paid additional salaries for their work coordinating SES. Parent coordinators distributed enrollment packets, fielded questions, and collected SES applications. Secretaries filed afterschool permits, food and nutrition workers prepared snacks, maintenance workers opened and maintained rooms, bus drivers reorganized their student rosters, and security officers staffed posts. Teachers allowed or refused afterschool instructors to teach SES in their rooms. Some daytime teachers gained employment with SES providers like United. Others contacted their union representatives, who in turn argued that union teachers should not work for SES providers, who were not paying into teacher pensions.

For their part, SES providers sent managers and their staffs to schools to recruit, train, and hire teachers. When allowed by the principals, they made marketing presentations at parent-teacher association meetings and school events. Often they arrived at seven in the morning to greet parents with marketing materials; they handed out flyers to parents who picked up their children after school; and placed promotional posters in local shops and businesses. When they could, without detection, they gave away thousands of dollars of incentives. These activities were all supported by the efforts of the office and warehouse staffs, who assembled the marketing materials, printed the flyers, and staffed the events. Others kept track of the event's attendees; they called parents who expressed interest in SES, and they paid those who staffed the events.

When SES programs actually began, the number of actors engaged in activity increased exponentially. Materials—teacher guides, student workbooks, tests, answer grids, notebooks, pens, pencils, chalk, and markers—were delivered, inventoried, stored, and then distributed to students and teachers. Program forms—rosters, sign-in sheets, sign-out sheets, classroom checklists, behavior forms, emergency plans, liability insurance certificates, contact lists, class lists, fax covers, and timesheets—were sorted and organized. Snacks were provided. Lessons were taught. Tests were administered. Rosters were collected. Students were disciplined and rewarded. Reports were generated. Parents were informed.

NCLB-guided toil was exerted across one association to the next. Many were repeated, especially once SES programs had begun. Others, such as marketing activities, were recycled as needed, where and when momentarily required. At the end of programs, most actions were suspended, although some were renewed. New motions ensured, as well. Some, such as those at Public School (PS) 472, were prematurely suspended and the associations were dissolved, although the events at the school were often referenced in United Education planning meetings. Most linkages, while temporary, persisted for the duration of one or two program cycles, if not longer.

Various actors, depending on their positionality within the emerging network, labored more intensively than others to secure continued relationships. United managers, who were monetarily rewarded, through promotions, salary, and annual bonuses, were motivated to renew contracts with schools. Throughout this book, we saw principals, who were heavily lobbied by the managers, resist their roles as SES "partners"—and having once accepted them, resisting the actions prescribed for them by NCLB. DOE administrators and staff of the state's education department also refused, at times, to regulate the implementation and over time, deferred to principals, further localizing greater autonomy and accountability of SES objectives.

Through their everyday actions, the policy stakeholders displayed not only that which was most important to them (McDermott and Varenne 2006, 25), but demonstrated that their agency had reflective capabilities. The interpretive work that actors performed was involved, temporarily, in the accountability of the action. Each actant had to make sense of what was expected; each had to know just enough of NCLB to, as Wittgenstein said, "know how to go on"—to play according to the new "rules" (Giddens 1979, 67). The work of interpreting and appropriating the rules was essentially linked to the rules themselves. However, what actors accomplished did not always match the directives and rules of NCLB. Rather, the rules were the medium of the production of practices—patterns of actions.

As actors appropriated the rules, they continually and reflexively monitored their actions, not only to keep up appearances (Goffman 1971), or play their assumed roles in the political spectacle of policy (Smith 2004) but also to make them accountable for practical purposes (Garfinkel 1967). Examining one of the paradoxical tenets of NCLB—having highly qualified teachers attend to failing children during the school day but having instructors who are not required to have any teaching experience attend to the same children in the SES program—illustrates these dual processes.

In an instance illustrated in chapter 5, a United instructor unable to demonstrate her skill at teaching eighth-grade English language arts curriculum skipped lessons and taught an entire session on the topic of genre based on her incorrect definition of the term. At times during the lesson she appeared, indeed, to be keeping up appearances for the students, who repeatedly questioned the correctness of her definition. As the instructor struggled to answer students' questions, she maintained her initial description of genre as the "generalities" or "general ideas" of a piece of writing. She was "passing" as someone who could teach the content. The instructor was also doing the work she had been hired to do and trying to make sense both of the lesson content and her position as an SES instructor attending to failing students, who knew more, on the topic of genre, than she did.

In the same chapter, a United instructor, a retired DOE teacher, who repeatedly instructed the students in her seventh-grade class to recite multiplication tables aloud even though it was not part of the curriculum and, more importantly, even though the students seemed to already have mastered them already. Making her actions reportable and logical, the instructor explained that "these kinds of kids"—those that attend failing schools—need to be taught the basics. Drawing on her years of experience as a DOE classroom teacher, she reasoned that her focus on single-digit multiplication table drills was essential.

Instructors were not the only United employees to take action. Other actors made "real" their knowledge and behaviors. The erroneous claims made by SES providers about the efficacy of their programs allowed the SES companies to pass off their programs as scientifically proven. Publicly making the assertions, which were replete with unsubstantiated and inflated findings, was essential in performing the part of a DOE partner; the claims made them worthy, under NCLB, of helping failing school children. Such performances allowed the providers to manage the actual lack of certainty and efficacy of their programs, which were not exactly proven and not exactly regulated.

NCLB drove the interface between actors and their environments. In some ways, the line between actors and their environments became blurred as actors were mandated to do different things with that which was already always there. In that interface zone, a space Martin (1997) refers to as "a field of constant response," change was required and actions took their shape in relation to the requirements of a continuously chang-ing environment, so that "their content, and even the terms in which they are understood, are also in constant change" (247). Often, the behavior of an actor depended not only on localizing NCLB, but also on the ac-tion of others, who were also localizing the policy and appropriating it in their daily environments. There existed an "interdependence of action" (Giddens 1979, 73) in which a change in one linkage also produced the potential for modification in one or more other linkages. Some changes were nearly self-contained, while others extended across the network. Environments were altered slightly, as well as radically, as responses to some changes quickly multiplied across linkages.

For example, when the newly adopted United Federation of Teach-ers (UFT) contract required that failing students receive an additional 37.5 minutes of small group instruction four days a week, parents, teach-ers, SES providers, bus drivers, security guards, and a host of others had to orient their actions toward the change. At United, operating procedures, program schedules, curriculum materials, and staffing budgets changed as a result of the additional sessions. Enrollment was also affected. Chil-dren were removed from United's afterschool program, which began 37.5 later, by parents who opposed the additional tutoring and the extended hours.

Like the action taken by the UFT, other acts directed at attending to failure could not be abstracted from the daily activities and actions of the everyday work of multiple actants. There existed many different cir-cumstances and situations that were considered and accounted for as "everyday." Because actors in this study occupied multiple levels of vari-ous organizations and topologies and did not necessarily share the same aims or interpretations of NCLB mandates, the response of one was often a potential sanction upon the acts of the others and vice versa (Parsons 1951, 1968).

In one of many examples, United sought to enroll as many students as possible; in contrast, many schools aimed to reduce their SES spending so that they could use their Title I funds for daytime educational supports. To increase the probability of enrolling large numbers of students, United targeted schools in which all students—usually 800–1,500—were eligible to receive SES. However, their actions were thwarted when a handful of principals, at universally eligible schools, attempted to minimize spending Title I funds on SES. One evoked an NCLB spending exemption, a "lack of demand" for SES to limit the number of SES participants to seventy. Another capped student enrollment at fifty, only to be challenged by parents, who wanted to enroll their children, and by teachers, who wanted to work in the SES program.

Again, it is obvious that while school failure represented the common point toward which activities were to be directed, the action flowed in multiple directions. It is hard to imagine it could be otherwise. Connections were made between entities in all sorts of configurations, creating a web of linkages. Actors operated simultaneously in multiple topologies, including United Education, failing schools, and local educational agencies. Most performed and behaved differently in different topologies depending on the group's relative position in the respective network. The aims of actors and agencies were often disparate and conflicting; and following the rules and "saving" one's job or organization often took precedence over, even when it intersected with, "leaving no child behind."

Failure was made to matter moment by moment, action by action, activity by activity, association by association, and topology by topology. It was made to matter differently—rendered consequential or not—by agents who were always actively making sense of their ever-changing circumstances afforded to them through the actions of local educational agencies, SES providers, and public schools. Much of making failure matter required a combination of—often conflicted—displays and performances of different inclinations and disinclinations within and between the topologies. Most presented themselves and performed as fully attentive to reducing or ending failure—of being fully oriented toward the "fetish" of failure.

United packaged itself in terms of a solution to failing students in failing schools. Organizationally, it minimally consisted of procedures by which to account for its ability to partner with failing schools to attend to those school's students. Some of the company's activities, such as hiring a few unskilled teachers and espousing unsubstantiated results, simultaneously suggested that not all their actions were intended to remedy failure. The conflict was this: United needed students and schools to fail in order to remain viable in the business of remedying failure. United, like other providers, selectively capitalized on failure's "popularity."

Recall that United was an "oligopticon" in the network, a location with a narrow but well-defined view. The for-profit tutoring sector examined in this study was problem focused. Money was made when proposed solutions to those problems were sold by the tutoring and testing companies to schools. Attending to failure—in its multiple semantic guises as "intervention," "remediation," and "customized curriculum"—provided these tutoring organizations with an ongoing and often lucrative project. NCLB propelled private tutoring and testing companies into what United's president described as an "upstream in profitability" (2008). During the years of this study, United's SES programs represented on average $4 million in annual revenue for the company. Operating in an open market and held to different standards than the public school system, United aimed to drive results that would be financially rewarding and stabilize or reinforce their organization.

School principals and their staff, too, selectively attended to failure. Individual schools in this research held the unique position in the network of both finding students failing and, in turn, being found as failing. They were to measure the failure of children, be measured by it, and then, according to NCLB measures, attend to it. Contestation and conflicts understandably arose from these complexities. Multiple instances examined in this study revealed that actions reflected the multiplicity in circumstances. Some, like the following example, showed how school administrators' actions seemed less than fully invested in attending to failure.

The principal and assistant principal of PS 472 publicly professed their commitment to doing as much as they could to end failure at their school. However, after the school provided United Education with teaching spaces and conditions that were unsafe, encouraged illegal billing, and neglected physical punishment used by an in-house community-based organization (CBO), United discontinued their program. Even as the principal and assistant principal refused to meet United's repeated requests for safe and adequate spaces, separate from the CBO's program, the principal continued to claim her administration needed United to help the school's failing kids. This led one of United's vice presidents to say of the school administrators at PS 472: "Well, at least they all drank the Kool-Aid. They're really on board with this No Child failure thing even if they aren't doing a damn thing about failing kids."

The principal at MS 532 was also "on board"—perhaps "overboard" in her enthusiasm for NCLB-mandate tutoring. Even though the school had met its adequate yearly progress (AYP) goals in all but one subject in one accountability group, the principal situated United, along with two other SES providers as the school's desperately needed "lifelines." Miscasting the school as a seriously failing school and in urgent need of outside help, the principal strongly encouraged, if not pressured, all of her students to enroll in SES. This resulted in a lower than average school environment rating, which was mostly calculated from family and teacher surveys, and it prompted more than fifty families to request transfers from the school. Both responses lowered the school's overall performance grade so that the school did actually need improvement.

Likewise, some DOE practices were instituted that hindered failing students from receiving academic support. There was an inconsistent and disorderly dispersal of SES enrollment forms. Schools reported shortages of enrollment packets, enrollment forms in languages that did not correspond with those of the student population, and deadlines that didn't allow them to adequately inform parents. Following their interpretation of SES mandates, DOE officials refused to supply additional forms, although some parent coordinators arbitrarily received additional packets. Numerous students who qualified and needed SES were left without a way to enroll in the program.

Grading and making public the scores for each school as required by NCLB, the DOE also decreased SES enrollments as principals, trying to improve their environment survey scores, diverted SES-eligible students into enrichment programs, aimed at increasing overall student, parent, and staff satisfaction. Torn between fulfilling their SES obligations, as defined by the position on the schools in need of improvement (SINI) list and taking aim at improving their overall grade, as required by DOE policies, some principals, for a variety of reasons, chose the latter, which often drew praise from parents who chose specific programs for their children. Paradoxically, the schools of most of the interviewed principals received grades of As and Bs, while simultaneously remaining in SINI status and, in some cases, moving toward restructuring. However, many schools proudly advertised their grades in newsletters, school reports, and parents meetings—and without exception, parents in this study spoke positively, if not proudly, of the "good" grades.

In contrast, SES, which was acclaimed by the federal and local educational authorities as a "parent-choice" program, drew mixed responses from parents. Parents were told in the parent packets and the enrollment guide that they were free to choose an SES provider whose program best met the needs of their children. However, in practice, when NCLB was appropriated locally, schools, not parents, entered into partnerships with SES providers to determine who provided services to students. Parent choice was undermined, if not ignored, as schools, not parents, signed contractual agreements with SES providers they had chosen. For children whose parents enrolled them with a provider that did not partner with their school, there was little recourse. The DOE had no effective way for parents to transfer children to other programs, and programs could not accept students who were enrolled in another provider's program. Those children who were not, according to NCLB, to be left behind did not receive services.

Culpability lied not solely in the actions of one DOE official who refused to provide additional enrollment forms any more than it lied exclusively with the actions of the principal who attempted to limit access to SES. However, each act provoked other actions, and together, they all colluded in furthering the problem. Making failure matter, in this sense, became the shared achievement of actants who were making sense of their circumstances in their everyday work, given the constraints of what was possible when failure is a prior condition that must be diligently fixed.

The participation of actors required that they achieve some "working consensus" about what they are doing (Goffman 1976). Raley (2006) suggests that such participation is a "more complex form of play" that challenges consensus and may be better phrased "working uncertainty" (161). In this ethnography, there existed constant effort in interactions to manage the uncertainty and achieve a minimal level of trust (McDermott 1977, 199). For instance, at Junior High School 345, the parents, assistant principal, and the principal stated that it was important for United to administer pretests to students; they expected it and wanted it. They did not care if the results were used diagnostically. United concurred. Pretest results were not used to restructure the scope or sequence of curriculum. This meant that even if all the students of one class correctly answered all the examination questions on, for instance, converting fractions, they would still be taught three lessons on converting fractions as prescribed in the standard United SES curriculum.

As shown, networks of relations were not intrinsically coherent. In an actor-network, objects and subjects did not "naturally" or "automatically" become some sort of "collective" without the processes of inscription—the process by which actors shape other actors' attributes and properties (Akrich and Latour 1997) and translation—the work of making dissimilar things with some corresponding attributes and properties similar. These processes were ceaselessly changing and iterative in nature, thus enabling a relative stability in the corresponding network even though groups of actants—SES providers and failing schools—had different "values" and procedural practices.

Much of what this book has illustrated is how actors came to share recognition of various forms of failure and, further, how they developed robust interventions and implemented action steps. They mutually defined the categorical distinctions of failure and continued to interpret the highly visible and consequential signs, like failing test scores and low marks on progress reports. Some are literally responsible for calculating the test scores and the AYPs. Many accepted the indicators as reliable "proof" that failure was indeed the problem to which many should attend. The particular version of school failure presented in NCLB and Children First was made to matter and circulated throughout the network.

Individual actants, macroactors, and groups of agents worked to maintain some practical everyday sense of attending to failure. Their labor also maintained the integrity of the actor-network. Relationships needed to be repeatedly "performed" for the network to stay intact. Thus, in the actor-network traced in this study, children were continually found to be failing; NCLB continually recognized them as failing; local educational agencies continually identified some public schools as failing; and tutoring and testing companies, like United, continually provided "solutions" to failure.

Further, to say that some actants—for instance, SES providers and school principals—were doing things is not to say that others—students, for example—were not also doing some thing(s). When actors acted together a netlike tracing was created. The space between the webbing represents not emptiness where nothing was happening, but networks in which many others were, by all assumptions, acting. Latour (2005) refers to this area as "plasma, namely that which has not yet formatted, not yet measured, not yet socialized, not yet engaged in metrological chains, and not yet covered, surveyed, mobilized, or subjectified" (244). The plasma of this study was full of potential actors and activities that had yet to be realized or enlisted for action in the SES network I traced.

Undoubtedly, children, teachers, parents, and many others were all working in those spaces. Many of the children had already been "noticed as fitting in an educational category" for children who learn less well (Varenne, Goldman, and McDermott 1998, 122). They were becoming acquired by a culture, by American education, which had grown preoccupied with noticing, diagnosing, and remedying their problem; they become the focus on which many adults were readily forcing their attentions (Varenne and McDermott 1998). All—the failing children and the adults who "help" them—were working hard with what had already, over time, been constructed.

McDermott and Varenne (2006) ask us to demonstrate our concern for the individual children while removing them as our unit of analysis or reorganization. They suggest that we look, instead, to culture with its power to arrange children's troubles. But where, exactly, should educational anthropologists look in educational processes to examine the organizing features of an active constitutive culture? Again, McDermott and Varenne point to possibilities: "To care for the children in trouble, the best action is not to diagnose them, but to reorganize the processes that made adults focus on the children and their received problems rather than on adults themselves. As researchers and policy-makers, and as teachers and parents interested in the best for every individual child, we should not allow isolation, diagnosis, and remediation to be our only recourse [—our only pattern for action]. Suppose we focus instead on the institutions that foreground each child's problem, including the institutions that place some of us seemingly in a position to help" (4). Look, they say, to educational institutions to examine the structuring powers of culture.

I say look "through" schools and "across" other educational institutions to educational policy culturally enacted. As one node in the NCLB actor-network, schools in this study are revealed to be loosely connected to a multitude of educational agencies across federal, state, and district, and also to community collectives and business organizations that are characteristically American. Educational policies like NCLB are "historical, arbitrary, and artificial, that is, are *cultural* in the best sense of the term" (McDermott and Varenne 2006, 4). Policy "drags" culture through educational institutions by the actions it prescribes and by the presumptions on which it gains purchase. "In contemporary American culture the linkages among governance, economics, and education are strong" (Smith 2004, 37) and yet educational policy is variably enacted and resisted. Because policy is appropriated differentially by various entities across an abundance of domains, it allows us to lose our "frames for what is to count as knowledge" (Varenne 2008, 359). As it is appropriated across institutions, policy carries with it culture's ability to enable and constrain actions—to organize circumstances in which children are found to be failing. As a mediator, it makes people act.

McDermott and Varenne (2006) say that "perhaps the biggest problem facing American education is that we foolishly await a solution" (29). I agree. There is no satisfying solution to school failure as it has been defined, and there is no resolution to the questions that have been asked about it. We must ask different questions, but first we must recognize that there have already been abundant solutions mandated by policies that have made failure matter even more. NCLB represents merely the latest. Policy solutions to school failure have paradoxically represented both a tendency toward continuity and conservation of values and practices—and also a desire for change and progression. The deployment of educational policy and reforms—the selection of goals and targets to achieve the goals, the designation of people and resources, and the project completion and establishment of task metrics—have mostly left school failure intact, if not strengthened, as an organizing concept and a focus of study.

Ethnographically Studying Educational Policy

Since Horace Mann proclaimed, "Education, beyond all other devices of human origin, is the equalizer of the conditions of men, the great balance wheel of social machinery" (Tyack 2001, 29), the public school system he envisioned has been the target of reform. For centuries, failing students have been cast as the problems to be remedied, and the country's public school system has remained central to public debates over how to define, construct, maintain, and remedy what has been framed by politicians, policy makers, and educators as a distinctly American way of life. Almost from their inception, public schools were seen as an antidote to social chaos, poverty, and social stratification—and the key to social improvement, cultural unity, and moral development. Wells (2006) notes that the United States has historically focused on educational achievement to improve society; America has "laid the task of rectifying societal inequalities at the schoolhouse door." NCLB legislates that this must remain so.

It is of little surprise that, in the twenty-first century, so many educational reformers and policy makers are still targeting schools for remediation. According to Reese (2005), "Adults who are unable to solve the nation's most serious, recurrent dilemmas—poverty, racial and social injustice, and civic apathy—predictably conclude that the solution resides not in their own behavior but in the flawed practices of the schools and imperfect nature of the young" (1–2). Moreover, many of those who have studied policy have treated it as an equalizing tool, studying it as a deliberate sequence of executive, administrative, adjudicative, and "official" texts that direct schools to improve failure.

NCLB has privileged quantitative data, like standardized achievement scores, over qualitative accounts of school experiences. Sleeter (2004) points out that the U.S. DOE now steers educators toward directives that attend not to the students' whole schooling experiences, but to strengthening students' achievement scores. She argues: "It is particularly ironic that federal legislation [NCLB] currently directs educators *away* from ethnography—away from insights based on ethnographic studies and away from use of qualitative inquiry as a tool to better understand local contexts and communities" (135). While the federal government, state and local educational agencies, and schools have leaned toward evidenced-based and research proven policy implementation, as illustrated here, the appropriation of policy is incredibly more complex, dynamic, and interactive than studies based solely on quantitative data and statistical analysis may suggest.

Shore and Wright (1997) note that rarely have anthropologists "turned their analytical gaze towards policy as a concept or cultural phenomenon" (7). The value of doing so—in treating policy as a "complex social practice, an ongoing process of normative cultural production" (Levinson and Sutton 2001, 1)—is imperative to an educational researcher. Studying NCLB ethnographically reveals the ways in which policy actively legitimizes the fetishism of school failure. It provides us with a powerful tool by which to challenge the culturally based meaning of social constructions that serve as the rationale and leverage for maintaining and explaining school failure. Ethnography is, after all, "radical activity" (McDermott 1987, 364).

I agree with Dixon, Borman, and Cotner (2009) who state that a "*perennial* challenge to anthropologists of education is the capacity to carve out a space within educational research as a whole that foregrounds the importance of understanding social processes that influence the ways individuals and groups affect and are affected by education policy mandates at different levels" (90). Moreover, I see the additional challenge for educational anthropologists as their willingness to study *policy itself* as a sociocultural process, in all its fluctuating manifestations, as it moves across systems, organizations, and institutions, both in and out of formal educational contexts. Interrogating what and who influences policy processes is important, but no more so than drawing attention to the everyday actions of those involved in making sense of the circumstances that are continually being shaped by—*and shaping*—policy processes. As Ball

(2006) reminds us: "It is one thing to consider the 'effects' of policies upon abstract social collectives" and quite another to capture the complexities and multiplicity of social actions and actors (22). Focusing on the ongoing interactions and associations, between multiple agents across diverse organizations, makes visible the tensions, contradictions, and incompatible aims that are necessarily translated and mediated.

This ethnography reveals the extent to which change, only some of which is directed toward the policy objective of fixing school failure, actually occurs. It dismantles the complexities of policy processes, laying bare the unintended consequences, and allows an investigation of the unanticipated results within the culturally constrained possibilities as they become vital linkages in the network. Localizing NCLB results in various problems for many people (not the least of which was making failure matter perhaps even more than it had before) so that many policy-informed actors can attend to it.

Shore (1997) states, "Anthropologists have long studied identity formation, ethnicity and nationalism as 'micro' or local-level phenomena" (165). An investigative focus on policy has the potential to provide a new avenue for studying the localization of global processes (Abu-Lugod 1990)—or as Latour (2005) contends, a localization of all processes. Actor-network theory, as employed in this study, connects the "macro" and the "micro" by localizing all action—local and "global" along ever-changing linkages. It provides a method for analyzing connections between levels and forms of process and action across multiple and varied locations.

Focusing on the flow of actions initiated when actors appropriate NCLB changes the field of study. It is no longer a question of studying school failure, but rather a study of what happens when the adults, some of whom have been making it an enormous problem, are provided with a policy "solution." Rather, the focus is on the social—the *non-priori* conditions, interactions, associations, and relations along which actions aimed at attending to school failure flow—and through which actors make their behaviors accountable in their everyday work situations.

Setting aside debates about what educational anthropology should and should not be, the ethnography of policy provides powerful possibilities for ways not to "solve" school failure, but instead to recast the actions of adult actors who direct their activities toward it. Studying educational policy ethnographically is to pay close attention to how the policy field is constructed and acted upon and to explore how adult actors work hard at making sense of the situations afforded to them by policy. It presents a method by which to disaggregate policy problematics, reveal policy performativities, and interrogate policy politics. Ethnographically examining policy processes and the problems that frame them is a way to make failure matter less by revealing how it came to such prominence and is maintained through the actions of adults, not children.

Policy study need not be a seriously compromised version of some anthropological ideal. In fact, committing to policy study as an educational anthropologist situates one in the position of removing culture as an undifferentiated residual category and integrating its complexities and furthering theoretical understandings, tensions, and contradictions in the policy field. Donnan and McFarlane (1997) explain:

> The environment in which anthropologists find themselves working is one where there is, perhaps inevitably, a skewed vision of what anthropology is "about" among policy professionals of other disciplines. In this environment, certain key words form part of a shared vocabulary, but the meanings attached to these words diverge radically between the different parties involved. As any anthropologist would expect, a term for which there are multiple meanings is "culture." For the policy professionals, and members of other disciplines, anthropologist are experts on "culture," but for the non-anthropologists who use and think about the term "culture," it still has the definitional attributes which anthropologists have been calling into question since at least the 1960s. For the non-anthropologists, "culture" seems to be thought of as a relatively discrete collection of essential or fundamental beliefs, values, assumptions and behavioral traits, passed on like a tradition from generation to generation, in only slowly changing form. (274–75)

Anthropologically studying educational policy must be taken as an important challenge to the discipline.

Working in conjunction with other disciplines on research that directly influences, if not drives, educational policy has often been seen as part of "the prescription for lifting anthropology out of its supposed states of theoretical malaise and ongoing crisis" (Donnan and McFarlane 1997, 261). Established scholars within anthropology have pushed for greater engagement with applied policy studies in order to expand the influence of anthropology; my position is slightly different. Simply, policy has increasingly assumed organizational and cultural roles in the lives of those who are, in some way, associated with American public schooling. Many educational anthropologists are, likely through our work, but also because of our circumstances outside of academia, linked to schools. In actor-network theory, those who study schooling are already a part of the flow of action in the network; our actions are already working on other associations and mediating the activities of other actors. It is clear that anthropologists informally contribute to educational policy processes through our professional and personal activities and behaviors.

On the other hand, our anthropologists' voices—which we mostly keep separate from our roles as educators, learners, parents of learners, and policy makers—are not often heard in policy-related research environments. Few policy projects and studies are initiated by anthropologists (Shore and Wright 1997), and those that are remain out of view of educational policy experts. There exists multiple intersecting issues, including limited access to decision makers, inadequate resources, and mismatched timing between ethnography and policy decisions that account for this lacuna in policy research. Ethnographic research, often conducted over months, if not years, is not recognized for its ability to respond timely enough to influence policy. However, educational policy, especially at the national and international levels, is often developed as the result of long-standing problems—such as school failure—and usually takes shape, as a document and sometimes a movement, over years, if not decades. Implementation takes even longer. The timeline in which to study the appropriation of policy is thus quite favorable for ethnographic methods. At their best, ethnographies illustrate the actual workings of policy in the day-to-day to illuminate, and I would argue, affect, the future experiences of children and adults impacted by the policy. Much can be learned by decision makers from ethnographies of policy.

Further, producing ethnographies of policy, which are mostly read by other policy researchers, need not be the only goal. Policy research should also be targeted to actors in policy processes. As educational researchers, it is important that we invest time in producing research summaries, policy briefs, statement papers, and essays "which generalize a way through the 'slippery intangibles' and complexity" (Donnan and McFarlane 1997, 278). In them, we may not be able to delve into the complexity of culture or the associations in an actor-network, but we can provide accurate and informative accounts of policy processes. We can tailor them to the emerging actor-networks in policy spheres. Academics who transform their work into more popular readings realize the difficulty of the task; they also see the practical benefits of their foray into unfamiliar genres. Educational anthropologists can find ways to enter our work and engage educators, students, and the general public in emerging forms of media, i.e., blogs, podcasts, and Web sites.[1] We continue to be well poised to share our knowledge on educational policy through publically sharing our work on "real life problems," such as school failure, by demystifying the policies that seek to alleviate them.

From this particular account of NCLB alone, we can say among many other things, that tests should be diagnostic and not punitive. Funding should be additive rather than subtractive. SES should be complementary instead of oppositional to school practices. Parents should be included and not excluded. Ultimate accountability should be to children, not to economic markets, educational agencies, or federal governments. More specifically, *Making Failure Pay* demonstrates that underfunding of NCLB critically affects the implementation of SES mandates at the school level by forcing principals to choose between spending their Title I funds on supplemental education for a comparatively small number of students—and not necessarily ones who are failing—and school-wide interventions and enrichment programs. It makes clear that federally mandating scientifically informed curricula, high-stakes testing, and strict accountability do not necessarily, if at all, result in measuring the complexity of what students learn and know. Rather, they result in a sanctions-driven accountability regime that elevates characterization, control, and comparison.

But underfunding and overtesting are, what Au (2009) calls "easy" NCLB targets, and these findings, if left to stand alone, would merely support a cacophony of voices from the academy, the government, and the public in urging dramatic changes in NCLB. Instead, I argue that this study not only criticizes the federal government's attempt to reduce failure, but more importantly prompts a rethinking/reframing/refocusing/resituating of the very target of NCLB. Federal policy intended to remedy school failure, a social achievement of many, need not be aimed at specific situations, particular behaviors, or isolated conditions of individuals or a select demographic group of children in need of intervention—which ultimately further characterizes some groups of learners as less than others. This book makes obvious that we do not even need children failing for many adults to accentuate, elaborate, and exaggerate failure.

I argue that failure is ubiquitous across the network because many actors have been working hard at making it matter. Sandage (2005) states that "failure stories are everywhere, if we can bear to hear them" (9). I heard, observed, and perhaps participated in the construction of more failure stories by asking why they were everywhere and why so many of us have stayed, looking in the same places, namely schools, to hear, see, and document more. The actions of so many—of adult agents and nonhuman actors—together made failure incredibly pervasive. Shore and Wright (1997) remind us: "It is a standard anthropological practice to focus on a concept that appears, to the people concerned, to be axiomatic and unproblematic, and to explore its different meanings and how it works as an organizing principle of society" (14). School failure, as demonstrated throughout this book, is complexly performed and enmeshed in multiple discourses composed of discordant voices.

Making Failure Pay is intended to be a generative and confrontational rendering of NCLB and school failure that invites readers to support, challenge, or dispel my concern that school failure has become so common as to be positioned as the American condition. It aims to relocate schools within their sociocultural environments and to find policy enmeshed in multiple social processes across multilayered contexts—and to provoke further investigations. It represents a struggling through my own uneasiness about portrayals of policy and school failure and ends now with the hope that it will, through readers' insights and interpretations, come to inhabit future policy conversations aimed at making failure pay much less.

NOTES

Chapter 1

1. Contested words like *problem, failure,* and *success* first appear in quote marks to indicate that they are a shared social achievement and as Varenne (2008) reminds us are "words we cannot escape but cannot take as given" (366).

2. Pseudonyms and generic position titles are used throughout. Exceptions include public figures, holding specific offices, who would be recognizable even with use of a pseudonym. However, I attribute only their public and publicized statements directly to them, without pseudonym.

3. The term "emerging bilinguals," proposed by Garcia (2009), more accurately characterizes students learning English when it is not their "mother tongue"; however, I use ELLs when referring to NCLB directives to maintain consistency with policy's language.

4. I prefer using "afterschool" to "after-school" in referring to the SES programs. I follow Noam, Biancarosa, and Dechausay (2002), who state that the term "afterschool" (one word) "conveys the institutional legitimacy of the field rather than a tangential add-on to the institution of school."

5. While the acronym SES has long been used, especially in the social sciences to denote socioeconomic status, it has been uniformly repurposed in federal, state, and local policy, as well as popular media, to designate NCLB's supplemental educational services. As well, actors in this study consistently referred to the supplemental tutoring as "SES." Even children in kindergarten and first grade were observed crying, "I don't want to go to SES!"

6. United Education is a pseudonym for a composite SES provider. I discuss the necessity and construction of United Education, in detail, later in this chapter. United is often used as an abbreviated form to refer to United Education.

7. This ethnography draws upon interviews, surveys, participation, observations, and document review across a field of policy-suggested interactions. NudistVivo 2.0 was used for data storage and gross analysis.

8. My positionality was reoriented during periods of the study in which I worked within the educational support industry, and I unquestionably became implicated in my cultural critique of NCLB processes. My "insider" status certainly enhanced my knowledge of privatization under NCLB and heightened my interest in SES, but it did not trump, substitute for, or disguise my role as educational anthropologist. Consents were obtained from study participants prior to interviews, observations, and document retrieval except for data collected at public events.

9. See, e.g., McDermott 1987; Lave and Wenger 1991; Levinson, Foley, and Holland 1996; Varenne and McDermott 1998; Holland and Lave 2001; Lave and McDermott 2002; Foley 2008.

10. As Latour's ideas and writings on actor-network theory have evolved, the theory's name has included two hyphens (actor-network-theory or ANT), one hyphen, and no hyphens. Of note, in 1999, he criticized the entire label, including the hyphens, but later, in 2005, he took the opposite position. I use "actor-network theory" to emphasize the linkages between actors in the network.

11. I was first introduced to the process of a script becoming a transcript in the work of James C. Scott (1990).

12. Marketing includes a variety of communications that are strictly regulated by NCLB—including but not limited to sending letters of inquiry to principals, meeting with principals and parent coordinators, attending parent-teacher association meetings, attending open houses, giving presentations, distributing materials to parents outside of schools, and participating in ongoing telephone, in-person, and electronic communications.

Chapter 2

1. See Stein (2004) for a thorough cultural analysis of ESEA.

2. Ninety-six percent of the nation's highest poverty schools (defined as those with 75 percent or greater students eligible for the free and reduced-price lunch program) receive nearly half of the Title I funds.

3. Nicknames for the policy reflect NCLB's divisive nature: No Child Left Untested, No School Board Left Standing, No Child's Behind Left, and No Child of Mine Left Behind are but a few.

4. By 2001, all fifty American states had both state learning standards and statewide assessments (Johnson and Johnson 2002, xviii), although the testing was often not aligned with the standards. By 2003, half the public school students in America were required to take additional graduation tests, and students in dozens of states were regularly tested for promotion (Wood 2004, 34).

5. According to NCLB: The AMO is the performance index (PI) value that signifies that an accountability group is making satisfactory progress toward the goal that 100 percent of students will be proficient in the state's learning standards for English language arts and mathematics by 2013–14. It combines the percentage of students who

partially met the state standard with the percentage of students who met or exceeded the standard. A PI is a value from 0 to 200 that is assigned to an accountability group, indicating how that group performed on a required state test. Student test scores on the tests are converted to four achievement levels, from level 1, indicating no proficiency, to level 4, indicating advanced proficiency. At the elementary and middle school levels, the PI is calculated with the following equation: $100 \times$ [(count of continuously enrolled tested students performing at levels 2, 3, and 4 + the count at levels 3 and 4) / count of all cohort members].

6. This pattern represents a strict adherence to NCLB; however, as shown throughout this study, there are many NCLB-sanctioned exceptions.

7. Prior to the middle of the nineteenth century, New York City authorities had assumed control of building a public school system. By 1900, the governance of the school system in the city had been centralized (Ravitch 2000).

8. The proposed reorganization, geared toward empowering principals, was presented to the principals when the administration was locked in a four-year-long contract dispute with principals and their union.

9. DOE Press Release ID N-42, 2006–2007, April, 16, 2007.

10. The DOE school assessment reports are not related to the state and federal legal assessments under NCLB.

11. SURR is a subset of SINI and non–Title I schools requiring academic progress (SRAP). Since its inception in 1989, 243 schools have received SURR designation. Of these, 116 improved enough to be removed from the list. In 2006, an all-time-low number of thirty-five schools were designated as SURR across the state. The reduction in number reflects the overriding accountability process of NCLB, not a reduction in "failing" schools.

12. Throughout the text, I use "actor," "agent," and "actant" interchangeably.

13. In Latour's (1987) theory, "translation" hints on its common usage in literacy and also as that of a connection that transports or moves thing from one place to another.

14. Opposite from the "panopticon" prison, where objectified person is seen but does not see and where he is the object of information never the subject in communication (Foucault 1979). Oligoptica are sites that do the opposite of panoptica.

Chapter 3

1. General sources for this chapter include NCLB (2001), New York City Department of Education's (DOE's) Web site at http://schools.nyc.gov/Administration/NCLB/SES, New York City DOE published materials, and briefs published by nonprofit and for-profit organizations, as well as educational research institutes. Specific references are cited throughout.

2. In Title I, Section 1116(e), the fifty-five-page federal nonregulatory guide for SES and also in the New York City DOE SES 2006–7 Provider Manual, the multiple roles and responsibilities of SES providers, schools, parents, the DOE, and the federal government are well delineated.

3. Privatization of educational programs in public schools, promoted by the educational reforms made after the publishing of *A Nation at Risk* (National Commission on Excellence in Education 1983), laid a foundation for an approach to school improvement focused on high-stakes testing and accountability—the cornerstones of NCLB and its predecessor Improving America's Schools Act (IASA) of 1994.

4. The "knowledge industry"—curriculum and testing—is a multimillion dollar industry. Toy manufacturer Milton Bradley began selling and profiting from instructional packets for kindergarteners in 1871; he was shortly joined by a multitude of organizations and companies, who sold their educational materials to schools across America. Today, the industry is controlled by relatively few major firms.

5. U.S. Government Accountability Office (U.S. GAO), http://www.gao.gov/new.items/d06758.pdf (accessed January 8, 2009).

6. In autumn 2007, the DOE stipulated in their contract with SES providers that programs must begin within thirty days of receiving enrollments.

7. SES providers are purposefully not identified by name in this section.

8. The same provider was later accused of falsifying enrollment forms, exaggerating enrollment numbers, doctoring student attendance data, and, according to the city's special commissioner of investigations report, the company over billed the city for $200,000.

9. Estimates of maximum per-pupil amount for SES are available at the U.S. Department of Education, http://www.ed.gov/about/overview/budget/titi/fy04/index.html-allocation (accessed February 2, 2005).

10. In 2005, the maximum per-child expenditure for SES was $2,193.37 in Brooklyn, $2,200.44 in the Bronx, $2,137.99 in Manhattan, and $2,145.70 in Queens. During 2005, the total Title I allocation for the Bronx was $222,618,905. Five percent of the total allocation, $44,523,781, was set aside for SES and school choice, and the per-child SES expenditure was calculated by dividing the set aside by the number of eligible students.

11. In 2006, only 3,025 of 24,563 eligible students in Washington, DC, received services because the district claimed it could afford no more.

12. "Parents, kids getting shut out of free help: Tutoring companies and advocates point to unkempt promise," February 17, 2006. CNN, http://www.cnn.com/2006/EDUCATION/02/17/school.tutors.ap/index.html (accessed February 21, 2006).

13. For an in depth examination of principals' actions, see Koyama (2009).

14. This book shows interest in the ways that testing process and then, later, test scores mediate NCLB actions, but test scores are not included in the analysis.

15. To evaluate their SES programs, as required by NCLB, the state of New Mexico used the pre- and posttest data provided by the SES vendors in their examination of SES effectiveness.

Chapter 4

1. DOE press release ID 377, October 3, 2005.

2. To see the full description and rules of adding the 150 minutes, see the "Guide to UFT Contract Changes," a memorandum distributed to principals by Dan Weisberg, the executive director of labor policy, November 29, 2005.

Chapter 5

1. There is no evidence, other than statements made by the principal at PS 427 that Great Works was, in fact, intending to become an approved SES provider. I obtained no verification from the state that Great Works had submitted an application.

2. The order of operations to be followed in solving mathematical expressions is as

follows: first, perform all the operations in parenthesis, then evaluate all exponents, next multiply, divide from left to right, and finally, add and subtract from left to right.

3. Three teachers continued their employment with United the following year; one was not invited back; and one left to pursue his acting career.

4. CNN.com, "Parents, kids getting shut out of free help: Tutoring companies and advocates point to unkempt promise," February 17, 2006.

5. Some schools are designated as "universal free lunch sites" for three years at a time. At these schools, all children are eligible to receive SES.

6. An NCLB/SES Action Brief, compiled by Public Education Network and the National Coalition for Parent Involvement in Education (2006) deconstructs the "parent-choice" provision. The brief states, "At the state level, parents must be consulted in order to promote participation by a greater variety of providers and to develop criteria for identifying high-quality providers [and] at the local level, parents must be able to choose *all* SES providers identified by the state that are within the geographical areas of the school district" (emphasis added, 5–6).

Chapter 6

1. Having cellular phones at public schools in New York City was banned, amid protests by parents, in 2007.

2. The site-specific information is drawn from the PS 100's 2004–5 annual school report, the region's 2003–4 annual regional report, and the New York City DOE's Parent Guide.

3. United's SES curriculum was not sold to schools. However, it was inadvertently sold to an SES provider, a competitor of United, in 2005. On numerous occasions, parents who enrolled their students in the competitor's program stated that their children were enrolled in United.

Chapter 7

1. See my Web site and blog, www.educationalanthropolicy.org, which attempts to integrate the work of educational anthropologists into policy conversations.

REFERENCES

Abu-Lugod, Lila. 1991. Writing against culture. In *Recapturing anthropology,* ed. Richard Fox, 137–62. Santa Fe, NM: School of American Research.

Adler, Margot. 2005. Growth spurt: The rise of tutoring in America. http://www.npr .org/templates/story/story/php?storyId=4676496 (accessed October 3, 2005).

Akrich, Madeline, and Bruno Latour. 1997. A summary of a convenient vocabulary for the semiotics of human and nonhuman assemblies. In *Shaping technology/building society,* ed. Wiebe E. Bijker and John Law, 259–64. Cambridge, MA: MIT Press.

Andreatta, David. 2007. N.Y. risks losing fed bucks for education. *New York Times,* January 9.

Anyon, Jean. 2005. *Radical possibilities: Public policy, urban education, and a new social movement.* New York: Routledge.

Ball, Stephen J. 1993. What is policy? Texts, trajectories and toolboxes. *Discourse* 13(2):10–17.

———. 1994. *Education reform: A critical and post-structural approach.* Buckingham, England: Open University Press.

———. 1998. Big policies/small world: An introduction to international perspectives in education. *Comparative Education* 34(2):119–30.

———. 2006. *Education policy and social class: The selected works of Stephen J. Ball.* World Library of EDUCATIONALISTS. London: Routledge.

———. 2008. *The education debate: Policy and politics in the twenty-first century.* Polity Press.

Bartlett, Lesley, M. Frederick, T. Gulbrandsen, and E. Murillo. 2002. The marketization of education: Public schools for private ends. *Anthropology and Education Quarterly* 33(1):5–29.

Behrent, Megan. 2009. Reclaiming our freedom to teach: Education reform in the Obama era. *Harvard Educational Review* 79(2):240–66.

Bijker, Wiebe E., and John Law, eds. 1997. *Shaping technology/building society: Studies in sociotechnical change.* Cambridge, MA: MIT Press.

Bloomberg, Michael R. 2007. The state of the city address. *Gotham Gazette: New York City News and Policy*, January 17. http://www.gothamgazette.com/article/searchlight/20070117/203/2080 (accessed September 6, 2007).

Burch, Patricia. 2009. *Hidden markets: The new educational privatization.* New York, NY: Routledge.

Burch, Patricia, Mathew Steinberg, and Joseph Donovan. 2007. Supplemental educational services and NCLB: Policy assumptions, market practices, emerging issues. *Educational Evaluation and Policy Analysis* 29(2):115–33.

Callon, Michael, and Bruno Latour. 1981. Unscrewing the big leviathan: How actors macro-structure reality and how sociologists help them to do so. In *Advances in social theory and methodology: Towards an integration of micro-and macro-sociologies*, ed. A. V. Circourel and K. Knorr-Cetina, 277–303. London: Routledge and Kegan Paul.

Chandler, Michael Alison. 2007. For teachers, being "highly qualified" is a subjective matter: "No Child" standards of content mastery widely interpreted. *Washington Post*, January 13.

Coburn, Cynthia E. 2005. The role of nonsystem actors in the relationship between policy and practice: The case of reading instruction in California. *Educational Evaluation and Policy Analysis* 27(1):23–52.

Condon, Richard. 2006a. Report prepared for Joel I. Klein, Chancellor, New York City Public Schools. Department of Investigation. Special Commissioner investigation case no. 2004-2153.

———. 2006b. Report Prepared for Joel I. Klein, Chancellor, New York City Public Schools. Department of Education. Special Commissioner investigation case no. 2006-0172.

Darling-Hammond, Linda. 2004. From "separate but equal" to "No Child Left Behind": The collision of new standards and old inequalities. In *Many children left behind: How the No Child Left Behind Act is damaging our children and our schools*, ed. Deborah Meier and George Wood, 3–32. Boston: Beacon Press.

———. 2009. President Obama and education: The possibility for dramatic improvements in teaching and learning. *Harvard Educational Review* 79(2):210–23.

Datnow, Amanda. 2006. Connections in the policy chain: The "co-construction" of implementation in comprehensive school reform. In *New directions in education policy implementation: Confronting complexity,* ed. Meredith I. Honig, 105–23. Albany: State University of New York Press.

Datnow, Amanda, L. Hubbard, and H. Mehan. 2002. *Extending educational reform: From one school to many.* London: Routledge Falmer Press.

de Certeau, Michel. 1984. *The practice of everyday life.* Berkeley: University of California Press.

Department of Education. 2005. Mayor Bloomberg announces tentative agreement with the United Federation of Teachers, October 3. Press ID 377. http://www

.nycboe.net/Administration/mediarelations/PressReleases/2005-2006/10032005
.htm (accessed October 7, 2005).

———. 2007. Schools Chancellor Klein announces new school support organizations to provide services to schools beginning in the 2007–08 school year. Press ID N-42, 2006-7. http://www.nycboe.net/Administration/mediarelations/PressReleases/2006–2007/04162007.htm (accessed April 17, 2007).

Dixon, Maressa L., Kathryn M. Borman, and Bridget A. Cotner. 2009. Current approaches to research in anthropology and education. In *Handbook of education policy research,* ed. Gary Sykes, Barbara Schneider, and David N. Plank, 83–92. New York: Routledge.

Donnan, Hastings, and Graham McFarlane. 1997. Anthropology and policy research: The view from Northern Ireland. In *Anthropology of policy: Critical perspectives on governance and power,* ed. Chris Shore and Susan Wright, 261–81. New York: Routledge.

Dumas, Michael J., and Jean Anyon. 2006. Toward a critical approach to education policy implementation. In *New directions in education policy implementation: Confronting complexity,* ed. Meredith I. Honig, 149–86. Albany: State University of New York Press.

Edelman, Murray. 1985. *The symbolic uses of politics.* Urbana: University of Illinois Press.

———. 1988. *Constructing the political spectacle.* Chicago: University of Chicago Press.

Elmore, Richard F., and Milbrey W. McLaughlin. 1982. Strategic choice in federal education policy: The compliance-assistance trade-off. In *Policy making in education: Eighty-first Yearbook of the National Society for the Study of Education,* ed. Ann Lieberman and Milbrey W. McLaughlin, 159–94. Chicago: University of Chicago Press.

Flynn, Margaret. 2002. Title I supplemental educational services and afterschool programs: Opportunities and challenges. The Finance Project. August. http://www.financeproject.org/osthome.htm (accessed October 20, 2009).

Foley, Doug. 2008. Questioning "cultural" explanations of classroom behaviors. In *Everyday antiracism: Getting real about race in school,* ed. Mica Pollock, 222–25. New York: New York Press.

Foucault, Michele. 1979. *Discipline and punish: The birth of the prison.* New York: Vintage Books.

Fuhrman, Susan H., ed. 1993. *Designing coherent education policy: Improving the system.* San Francisco: Jossey-Bass Publishers.

Garcia, Ofelía. 2009. *Bilingual education in the 21st century: A global perspective.* Oxford: Wiley-Blackwell.

Garfinkel, Harold. 1967. *Studies of ethnomethodology.* Cambridge: Polity Press.

Giddens, Anthony. 1979. *Central problems in social theory: Action, structure and contradiction in social analysis.* Berkeley: University of California Press.

Giroux, Henry A. 2009. Obama's dilemma: Postpartisan politics and the crisis of American education. *Harvard Educational Review* 79(2):250–66.

Goffman, Erving. 1959. *The presentation of self in everyday life.* Garden City, NY: Doubleday Anchor Books.

———. 1976. *Relations in public.* New York: Harper and Row, Publishers, Inc.

Government Accountability Office (GAO). 2006. *No Child Left Behind Act: Education actions needed to improve local implementation and state evaluation of supplemental educational services.* Washington, DC: GAO Report 06-758.

Hamann, Edmund, and Brett Lane. 2004. The roles of state departments of education as policy intermediaries: Two cases. *Educational Policy* 18(3):426–55.

Heinrich, Carolyn. (2009). Third-party governance under No Child Left Behind: Accountability and performance management challenges. La Follette School Working Paper No. 2009-011. Madison, WI: Robert M. La Follette School of Public Affairs.

Heinrich, Carolyn J., Robert H. Meyer, and Gregory W. Whitten. 2009. Supplemental education services under No Child Left Behind: Who signs up, and what do they gain? La Follette School Working Paper No. 2009-010. Madison, WI: Robert M. La Follette School of Public Affairs.

Herszenhorn, David M. 2006a. New tutoring schedules in schools lead to confusions. *New York Times*, February 7.

———. 2006b. N.Y. English scores drop sharply in 6th grade. *New York Times*, September 22.

———. 2006c. Manhattan: Tutoring contract suspended. *New York Times*, October 26.

———. 2007. Respect is nice, but principals want raise. *New York Times*, January 29.

Holland, Dorothy, and Jean Lave, eds. 2001. History in person: Enduring struggles, contentious practice, intimate identities. Santa Fe, NM: School of American Research.

Honig, Meredith I. 2006a. Complexity and policy implementation: Challenges and opportunities for the field. In *New directions in education policy implementation: Confronting complexity,* ed. Meredith I. Honig, 1–23. Albany: State University of New York Press.

———. 2006b. Building policy from practice: Implementation as organizational learning. In *New directions in education policy implementation: Confronting complexity,* ed. Meredith I. Honig, 125–47. Albany: State University of New York Press.

Johnson, Dale D., and Bonnie Johnson. 2002. High stakes: Children, testing, and failure in American schools. New York: Rowman and Littlefield Publishers, Inc.

Karp, Stan. 2004. NCLB and democracy. In *Many children left behind: How the No Child Left Behind Act is damaging our children and our schools,* ed. Deborah Meier and George Wood, 53–65. Boston: Beacon Press.

Kim, James, and Gail L. Sunderland. 2005. Measuring academic proficiency under the No Child Left Behind Act: Implications for educational equity. *Educational Researcher* 34(8):3–13.

Klein, Joel. 2007. Chancellor Klein's prepared remarks to the partnership for New York City on the next phase of children first school reforms. http://schools.nyc.gov/Administration/mediarelations/SpeechesTestimony (accessed January 22, 2007).

Kohn, Alfie. 2004. NCLB and the effort to privatize public education. In *Many children left behind: How the No Child Left Behind Act is damaging our children and our schools,* ed. Deborah Meier and George Wood, 79–97. Boston: Beacon Press.

Koyama, Jill P. 2009. Localizing No Child Left Behind: Supplemental educational services (SES) in New York City. In *Comparatively knowing: Vertical case study research in comparative and development education,* ed. Francis Vavrus and Lesley Bartlett. New York: Palgrave Macmillan.

———. Forthcoming. "Supplemental educational services" (SES): NCLB's extended school day. In *Perspectives on comprehensive education,* vol. 3, ed. Hervé Varenne, Edmund Gordon, and Linda Lin. Lewiston, NY: Edwin Mellen Press.

Latour, Bruno. 1987. *Science in action: How to follow scientists and engineers through society.* Cambridge, MA: Harvard University Press.

———. 1993. *We have never been modern.* Cambridge, MA: Harvard University Press.

———. 1995. Social theory and the study of computerized work sites. In *Information technology and changes in organizational work,* ed. N. J. Orlinokowski and Geoff Walsham, 295–307. London: Chapman and Hall.

———. 1997. A well-articulated primatology—reflections of a fellow-traveler. In *Primate encounters,* ed. Shirley Strum and Linda Fedigan, 358–81. Chicago: University of Chicago Press.

———. 1999. On recalling ANT. In *Actor network theory and after,* ed. John Law and J. Hassard, 5–25. Malden, MA: Blackwell.

———. 2005. *Reassembling the social: An introduction to actor-network-theory.* Oxford: Oxford University Press.

Lave, Jean, and Ray McDermott. 2002. Estranged labor learning. *Outlines* 4:19–48.

Lave, Jean, and Etienne Wenger. 1991. *Situated learning: Legitimate peripheral participation.* Cambridge: Cambridge University Press.

Lee Jaekyung. 2008. Two takes on the impact of NCLB on academic improvement: Tracking sate proficiency trends through NAEP versus state assessments. In *Holding NCLB accountable: Achieving accountability, equity, & school reform,* ed. Gail L. Sunderman, 75–89. Thousand Oaks, CA: Corwin Press.

Levinson, Bradley A., D. E. Foley, and D. C. Holland. 1996. *The cultural production of the educated person.* Albany: State University of New York Press.

Levinson, Bradley A. U., and Margaret Sutton. 2001. Introduction: Policy as/in practice—a sociocultural approach to the study of educational policy. In *Policy as practice: Toward a comparative sociocultural analysis of educational policy,* ed. Margaret Sutton and Bradley A. U. Levinson, 1–22. Westport, CN: Ablex Publishing.

Linn, Robert L. 2008. Toward a more effective definition of adequate yearly progress. In *Holding NCLB accountable: Achieving accountability, equity, & school reform,* ed. Gail L. Sunderman, 27–42. Thousand Oaks, CA: Corwin Press.

Lipman, Pauline. 2000. Bush's education plan, globalization, and two politics of race. *Cultural Logic* 4(1). http://clogic.eserver.org/4–1/lipman.html (accessed January 10, 2004).

———. 2004. *High-stakes education: Inequality, globalization, and urban school reform.* New York: Routledge Falmer.

Loder, Tandra L. 2006. Why we can't leave public schools behind: The inseparable legacy of public education and American democracy. *Educational Researcher* 35(5):30–35.

Malen, Betty. 2006. Revisiting policy implementation as a political phenomenon: The case of reconstruction policies. In *New directions in education policy implementation: Confronting complexity,* ed. Meredith I. Honig, 83–104. Albany: State University of New York Press.

Manicka, Rani. 2003. *The rice mother.* New York: Penguin Books.

Marcus, George E., and Michael M. J. Fischer. 1999. *Anthropology as cultural critique: An experimental moment in the human sciences.* 2nd ed. Chicago: University of Chicago Press.

Margalit, Avishai. 2002. *The ethics of memory.* Cambridge, MA: Harvard University Press.

Martin, Emily. 1997. Managing Americans: policy and changes in the meaning of work and the self. In *Anthropology of policy: Critical perspectives on governance and power,* ed. Chris Shore and Susan Wright, 239–57. New York: Routledge.

Mathis, William. 2003. No Child Left Behind: Costs and benefits. *Phi Delta Kappan,* May.

McDermott, Kathryn A. 2007. "Expanding the moral community" or "blaming the victim"? The politics of state education accountability policy. *American Educational Research Journal* 44(1):77–111.

McDermott, Ray P. 1977. Social relations as contexts for learning in school. *Harvard Educational Review* 47(2):198–213.

———. 1987. The explanation of minority school failure, again. *Anthropology and Education Quarterly* 18:361–67.

McDermott, Ray P., and Kathleen D. Hall. 2007. Scientifically debased research on learning, 1854–2006. *Anthropology and Education Quarterly* 38(1):9–15.

McDermott, Ray, and Hervé Varenne. 2006. Reconstructing culture in educational research. In *Innovations in educational ethnography: Theory, methods, and results,* ed. George Spindler and Lorie Hammond, 3–31. Mahwah, NJ: Lawrence Erlbaum.

McLaughlin, Milbrey W. 2006. Implementation research in education: Lessons learned, lingering questions and new opportunities In *New directions in education policy implementation: Confronting complexity,* ed. Meredith I. Honig, 209–28. Albany: State University of New York Press.

McNeil, Linda. 2005. Faking equity: High stakes testing and the education of Latino youth. In *Leaving children behind: How "Texas-style" accountability fails Latino youth,* ed. Angela Velenauela, 7–111. Albany: State University of New York Press.

Medina, Jennifer. 2008 Cost of grading schools is said to be $130 million. *New York Times,* November 14, A29.

Mintrop, Heinrich, and Gail L. Sunderman. 2009. Predictable failure of federal sanctions-driven accountability for school improvement and why we may retain it anyway. *Educational Researcher* 38(4):353–64.

Molnar, Alex. 2005. *School commercialism: From democratic ideal to market commodity.* New York: Routledge.

Muñoz, Marco A., and Steven M. Ross. 2009. Supplemental educational services as a component of No Child Left Behind: A mixed-method analysis of its impact on student achievement. National Center for the Study of Privatization in Education. Occasional Paper No. 177. http://www.ncspe.org/publications_files/OP177.pdf (accessed October 15, 2009).

Nader, Laura. 1974. Up the anthropologist—perspectives gained from studying up. In *Reinventing anthropology,* ed. Dell Hymes. New York: Random House.

National Commission on Excellence in Education. 1983. *A Nation at risk: The imperative for educational reform.* Washington, DC: U.S. Department of Education.

New York City Department of Education. 2005. Summary of public schools choice program for elementary and middles schools students under No Child Left Behind. http://www.nycenet.edu/Administration/mediarelations/PressReleases/2004-2005/2-18-2005-15-6-48-326.htm (accessed March 19, 2005).

New York Times. 2007. Editorial: New York's public schools. January 28.

Noam, Gil G., G. Biancarosa, and N. Dechausay. 2003. *Afterschool education: Approaches to an emerging field.* Cambridge, MA: Harvard Education Press.

Novak, J. R., and Barbara A. Fuller. 2003. Penalizing diverse schools? Policy brief 03–4. Berkeley: Policy Analysis for California Education. http://pace.berkeley.edu/policy_brief_03–4_Pen.Div.pdf (accessed May 9, 2006).

O'Day, Jennifer A. 2002. Complexity, accountability, and school improvement. *Harvard Educational Review* 72(3):1–31.

Olsen, Brad, and Dena Sexton (2009). Threat rigidity, school reform, and how teachers view their work inside current education policy contexts. *American Educational Research Journal* 46(1):9–44.

Ortner, Sherry B. 1994. Theory in anthropology since the sixties. In *Culture/power/history: A reader in contemporary social theory*, ed. Nicholas. B. Dirks, Geoff. Eley, and Sherry B. Ortner, 372–410. Princeton, NJ: Princeton University Press.

Ortner, Sherry B. *New Jersey dreaming: Capital, culture, and the class of '58*. Durham, NC: Duke University Press.

Ozga, Jenny. 1987. Studying education policy through lives of policy makers. In *Changing policies, changing teachers*, ed. Stephen Walker and Len Barton. Philadelphia: Open University Press.

Parsons, Talcott. 1951. *The social system*. New York: Free Press.

———, ed. 1968. *American sociology: Perspectives, problems, methods*. New York: Basic Books.

Pennington, Julie L. 2004. *The colonization of literacy education: A story of reading in one elementary school*. New York: Peter Lang.

Peterson, Paul E. 2005. Making up the rules as you play the game: A conflict of interest at the very heart of NCLB. *Education Next* 5(4):42–49.

Rabinow, Paul, and George E. Marcus, with James D. Faubion and Tobias Rees. 2008. *Designs for an anthropology of the contemporary*. Durham, NC: Duke University Press.

Raley, Jason Duque. 2006. Finding safety in dangerous places: From *micro* to *micro* and back again. In *Innovations in educational ethnography: Theory, methods, and research*, ed. George Spindler and Lorie Hammond, 127–67. Mahwah, NJ: Lawrence Erlbaum Associates.

Ravitch, Diane. 2000. *The great school wars: A history of the New York City public schools*. Baltimore: The Johns Hopkins University Press.

Reese, William J. 2005. *America's public schools: From the common school to "No Child Left Behind."* Baltimore: Johns Hopkins University Press.

Reinhold, Susan. 1994. Local conflict and ideological struggle: "Positive images" and "section 28." PhD dissertation, University of Sussex.

Rickles, Jordan H. and Melissa K. Barnhart. 2007. The impact of supplemental educational services participation on student achievement: 2005–06. Report of the Los Angeles Unified School District Program Evaluation and Research Branch, Planning, Assessment and Research Division Publication No. 352.

Ross, Steven M., Jennifer Harmon, and Kenneth Wong, with Janis Langdon, Lynn Harrison, James Ford, and Laura L. Neergaard. 2009. Improving SES quality: State approval, monitoring, and evaluation of SES providers. Lincoln, IL: Academic Development Institute, Center on Innovation and Improvement.

Ryan, Susan, and Serah Fatani. 2005. SES Tutoring programs: An evaluation of the second year—part one of a two part report. Policy report, Office of Research, Evaluation and Accountability, Chicago Public Schools, Chicago.

Salinas, Cinthia S. 2007. The cultural politics of the Texas educational reform agenda: Examining who gets what, when, and how. *Anthropology and Education Quarterly* 38:42–56.

Sandage, Scott A. 2005. *Born losers: A history of failure in America*. Cambridge, MA: Harvard University Press.

Saulny, Susan. 2005a. Teachers' union is approved for U.S. tutoring program. *New York Times,* March 19.

———. 2005b. A lucrative brand of tutoring grows unchecked. *New York Times,* April 4.

Saussure, Ferdinand de. 1983. *Course in general linguistics.* La Salle, IL: Open Court Publishing Company.

Schemo, Diana Jean. 2007. Democrats push for changes to No Child left Behind law. *New York Times,* January 8.

Scott, James C. 1990. *Domination and the arts of resistance: Hidden transcripts.* New Haven, CT: Yale University Press.

Scott, W. Richard. 2008. *Institutions and organizations: Ideas and interests.* 3rd ed. Los Angeles: Sage Publications.

Shore, Cris. 1997. Governing Europe: European Union audiovisual policy and the politics of identity. In *Anthropology of policy: Critical perspectives on governance and power,* ed. Chris Shore and Susan Wright, 65–192. New York: Routledge.

Shore, Cris, and Susan Wright, eds. 1997. *Anthropology of policy: Critical perspectives on governance and power.* New York: Routledge.

Sizer, Theodore R. 1984. *Horace's compromise: The dilemma of American high school.* New York: Houghton Mifflin.

———. 1992. *Horace's school: Redesigning the America high school.* New York: Houghton Mifflin.

———. 1997. *Horace's hope: What works for the American high school.* New York: Houghton Mifflin.

———. 2004. Preamble: A reminder for Americans. In *Many children left behind: How the No Child Left Behind Act is damaging our children and our schools,* ed. Deborah Meier and George Wood, xvii–xxii. Boston: Beacon Press.

Sleeter, Christine E. 2004. Context-conscious portraits and context-blind policy. *Anthropology and Education Quarterly* 35(1):132–36.

Smith, Marshall, and Jennifer A. O'Day. 1991. *Putting the pieces together: Systemic school reform.* CPRE Policy Brief. New Brunswick, NJ: Eagleton Institute of Politics.

Smith, Mary Lee, with Linda Miller-Kahn, Walter Heinecke, and Patricia F. Jarvis. 2004. *Political spectacle and the fate of American schools.* New York: Routledge.

Sunderman, Gail L., ed. 2008. Holding NCLB accountable: Achieving accountability, equity, & school reform. Thousand Oaks, CA: Corwin Press.

Sunderman, Gail L., J. Kim, and G. Orfield. 2005. *NCLB meets school realities: Lessons from the field.* Thousand Oaks, CA: Corwin Press.

Spillane, James P., L. M. Gomez, and L. Mesler 2009. Notes on reframing the role of organizations in policy implementation: Resources for practice, in practice. In *Handbook of education policy research,* ed. Gary Sykes, Barbara Schneider, and David N. Plank, 409–25. New York: Routledge.

Stein, Sandra J. 2004. *The culture of education policy.* New York: Teachers College Press.

Sunderman, Gail L. 2007a. *Holding NCLB accountability: Achieving accountability, equity, and school reform.* Thousand Oaks, CA: Corwin Press.

———. 2007b. Policy brief. Supplemental educational services under NCLB: Charting implementation. Los Angeles: Civil Rights Project, UCLA.

Sunderman, Gail L., and Gary Orfield. 2006. Domesticating a revolution: No Child Left Behind and state administrative response. *Harvard Educational Review* 76(4): 526–56.

Taddei, Renzo Romano. 2005. Of clouds and streams, prophets and profits: The political semiotics of climate and water in the Brazilian northeast. PhD dissertation, Department of International and Transcultural Studies, Teachers College, Columbia University.

Taylor, James R., and Elizabeth J. Van Every, eds. 2000. *The emergent organization: Communication as its site and surface.* Mahway, NJ: Lawrence Erlbaum.

Traub, James. 2003. New York's new approach. http://www.nytimes.com/2003/08/03/edlife/03EDTRAUB.html?ei= (accessed June 29, 2007).

———. 2005. Bloomberg's city: Politics in an era of anticlimax. *New York Times Magazine,* October 2, 21–25.

Tyack, David. 2001. *School: The story of American public education.* Boston: Beacon Press.

U.S. Department of Education. 2001. No Child Left Behind Act of 2001. http://www.ed.gov/nclb/landing.jhtml (accessed March 3, 2005).

Valenzuela, Angela. 1999. Subtractive schooling: U.S.-Mexican youth and the politics of caring. New York: State University of New York Press.

Varenne, Hervé. 2007. Difficult collective deliberations: Anthropological notes toward a theory of education. *Teachers College Record* 109(7):1559–87.

———. 2008. Reflections from the field: Culture, education, anthropology. *Anthropology and Education Quarterly* 39(4):356–68.

Varenne, Hervé, S. Goldman, and R. McDermott. 1998. Racing in place. In *Successful failure: The school America builds,* ed. Hervé Varenne and Ray McDermott, 106–28. Boulder, CO: Westview.

Varenne, Hervé, and Ray McDermott. 1998. *Successful failure: The school America builds.* Boulder, CO: Westview.

Vavrus, Francis, and Lesley Bartlett, eds. 2009. *Comparatively knowing: Vertical case study research in comparative and development education.* New York: Palgrave Macmillan.

Weiss, Beth M. 2005. Teachers, unions, and commercialism. In *Many children left behind: How the No Child Left Behind Act is damaging our children and our schools,* ed. Deborah Meier and George Wood, 69–81. Boston: Beacon Press.

Wells, Amy Stuart. 2006. Our children's burden: A history of federal education policies that ask (now require) our public schools to solve social inequality. Opening remarks at the Campaign for Educational Equity Symposium, Fall 2006, Teachers College, Columbia University, November 13–14.

Williams, Juliet. 2007. California at odds with feds over No Child Left Behind law. Associated Press Newswires, January 17.

Williams, Raymond. 1976. *Keywords: A vocabulary of culture and society.* New York: Oxford University Press.

Willis, Paul, and Mats Trondman. 2000. Manifesto for ethnography. *Ethnography* 1(1):5–16.

Wood, George. 2004. A view from the field: NCLB's effects on classrooms and schools. In *Many children left behind: How the No Child Left Behind Act is damaging our children and our schools,* ed. Deborah Meier and George Wood, 33–50. Boston: Beacon Press.

Wright, Susan. 1994. *Anthropology of organizations.* London: Routledge.

Zimmerman, Ron, B. Gill, P. Razquin, K. Booker, and J. R. Lockwood III. 2007. *State and local implementation of the No Child Left Behind Act: Volume I—Title I school choice, supplemental educational services, and student achievement.* Washington, DC: RAND.

INDEX